THE WORD ON THE STREET

THE WORD ON THE STREET

The Unsanctioned Story of Oasis

EUGENE MASTERSON

EDINBURGH AND LONDON

PICTURE CREDITS

Cathal Dawson – p.20, p.21, p.29, p.33, p.36, p.44, p.51, p.53, p.57, p.61, p.64, p.85, p.89, p.93

Neil Fraser – cover, p.17, p.42, p.43, p.62, p.73, p.74, p.76, p.79, p.80, p.83, p.90

Kyran O'Brien – p.24, p.26, p.27, p.58, p.66, p.69, p.87

Rex Features – p.18, p.23, p.30, p.35, p.39, p.40, p.41, p.46, p.47, p.49, p.55, p.70, p.95

Courtesy of Gallagher family (Ireland) and John Moore/News Group International – p.7, p.8, p.9, p.10, p.11, p.12, p.14, p.15

Every effort has been made to credit the copyright holders of the photographs in this book. The publishers apologise if, by being unable to trace any sources, we have unknowingly failed to acknowledge ownership.

First published in Great Britain in 1996 by
MAINSTREAM PUBLISHING COMPANY (EDINBURGH) LTD
7 Albany Street
Edinburgh EH1 3UG

ISBN 1 85158 890 6

A catalogue for this book is available from the British Library

Designed by Andrew Laycock

Typeset in Gill Sans
Printed and bound in Great Britain by Bath Press ColourBooks, Blantyre

Contents

Growing up in Burnage

Oasis's roots lie in the bleak south Manchester suburb of Burnage where they experienced an ordinary working-class upbringing. The original band line-up shares with that other great Manchester band, The Smiths, the intriguing connection of Irish roots. Most members of both bands derive from Irish emigrants who fled their mother country in the 1950s and 1960s to seek work in the then industrial hub of Manchester.

All four members of The Smiths had parents who hailed from Ireland, which is hardly surprising given their names: Stephen Patrick Morrisey, Mike Joyce, Andy Smith and John Maher (he later changed his surname to the more pronounceable 'Marr'). The Gallagher brothers' parents also originated in Ireland. Their mother, Margaret, more commonly known as Peggy, came from the quiet west of Ireland town of Charlestown in Co. Mayo while their father, Tommy, grew up in the village of Duleek, Co. Meath, not far from Dublin.

The other three original members of Oasis, Paul 'Guigsy' McGuigan, Paul 'Bonehead' Arthurs and Tony McCarroll, also had Irish roots, but more distant than the Gallaghers. Replacement member Alan White is believed to have no Irish heritage. So it was with more than a touch of irony that the 'Irish mafia' link in Manchester should prove so important in Oasis's ascent. For it was Johnny Marr who became so enthused after hearing a demo tape that he contacted Noel and eventually persuaded his manager, Marcus Russell, to take over at the helm of the fledgling Oasis.

The Gallaghers themselves grew up in Burnage, a dreary area sometimes referred to as 'Boring Burnage'. Noel was born on 29 May 1967, while Liam was born 'William' on 21 September 1972 (he later shortened his name to the Irish version of 'Liam'). They have an older

Noel, Paul and Liam stand up beside that fireplace in 1974 with Mum Peggy.

A cute white-haired Noel as a toddler (left) with brother Paul on holiday in Ireland in the early '70s.

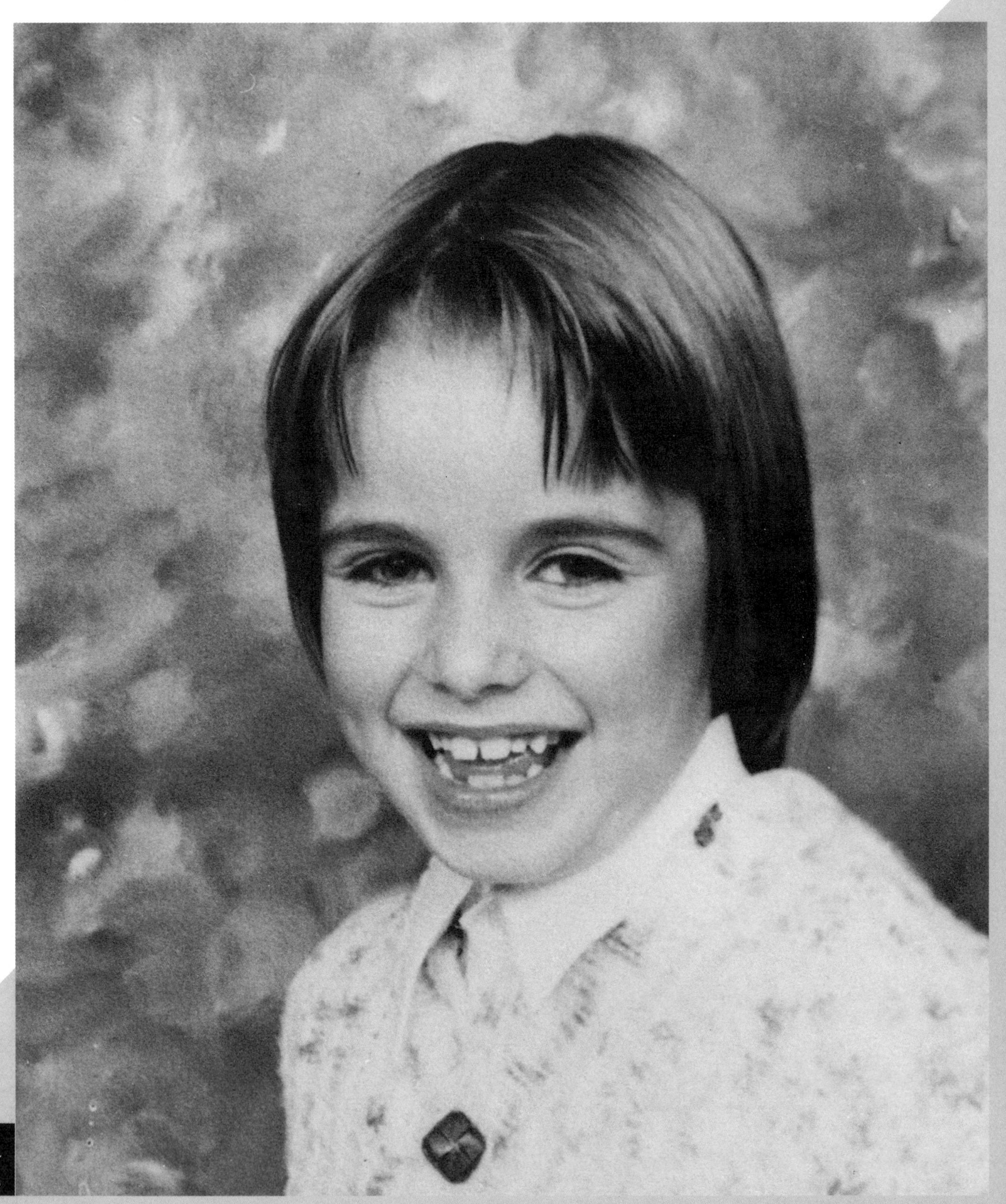

Angelic Liam manages a smile.

Schoolboy Noel shows off his future hairstyle!

brother, Paul, born in 1965, who still lives in their family home in Burnage.

Liam's only interest at school was in football but he often played truant and sniffed glue. He'd later tell the *Sunday Times*: 'I sniffed cans of gas at the age of 12, took magic mushrooms at the age of 12. Not 20 mushrooms, more like 150.' He left school without a qualification but while there he strangely took an interest in learning the violin at music classes. Noel's schooldays also involved a lot of truancy, smoking marijuana ('draw') and sniffing glue. When he too left with no qualifications a careers officer said he'd end up working at the local McVitie's biscuit factory, where his Mum used to toil away.

Tommy formed his own Under-14 Gaelic football team and Noel recalls scoring a point in Croke Park in Dublin during a schools tournament. The brothers are still fans of the Meath County Gaelic football team in Ireland. They were also cub scouts and they made their debut stage appearances in their annual school nativity plays at St Bernard's Roman Catholic primary school in Burnage with Liam once donning a fluffy suit to play the part of a lamb!

Both brothers had run-ins with the law in their early days. Noel was put on probation when he was caught robbing a local corner shop at the age of 16 while Liam's only known misdemeanours involved driving cars and motorbikes without insurance.

[T]he Gallagher boys at a family [w]edding in Ireland circa 1973. [T]heir estranged father Tommy [i]s holding Noel.

Their parents used to bring the whole family to Ireland every year. 'Until I was about 15, myself and my two brothers would spend six weeks every year and three weeks every Christmas in Mayo,' Noel recalls. 'That's a lot of time when you're a child. The town in Mayo had a church, a post office and about 300 pubs. It was all farmland and I was a bit freaked out by all the sheep and the cows because I was from Manchester. We'd never seen the likes of nettles and fields and stacks of hay and all that. But it was great – the three of us used to go fishing all the time. Our cousins there never dared laugh at our English accents because they would have got a clip around the ear if they did. It was a great childhood and it's something I talk a lot about to Johnny Marr, who had a similar upbringing.

'Me Mam was determined to give us some Irish culture 'cause we were used to concrete flats and stuff. It was a bit of a culture shock for the first four or five years but we just grew to love it. I still do to this day and the great thing about coming to Ireland is at the airport when you know that smell in the air is turf burning. It almost brings a tear to your eye.

Day out with Dad

'I think that being brought up an Irish Catholic is both the best and worst way of being brought up. The whole thing is all that religion bollocks, which I don't go for at all. The best thing is the culture, particularly the music. I mean, I really don't particularly like ceilidh music, it's not my cup of tea, but at least I can understand where it's coming from. I really believe that the whole Irish Catholic thing does shape the way you view the world. I still have this guilt thing, it never really leaves you. But then I think I have it less than my parents and the next generation will have it less than me, so maybe it will just wither out.'

Their early jobs were pretty manual and a lot of their teenage years were spent on building sites as labourers, mainly with their dad. He owned his own business, laying down concrete floors, and the three brothers, their dad and a couple of uncles and cousins used to turn up to work in a yellow transit van and toil away till late at night. There were lots of arguments among the siblings in those days too, and Noel says they were a type of 'Burnage Hillbillies'. Many of Noel's and Liam's jobs were part time on Saturday and Noel also spent time as a signwriter for an estate agent, was a baker, worked in a bed factory and was even a fish tank maker. Liam spent time as a car valet and signed on the dole for four years before Oasis took off (his friends jokingly nicknamed him 'Doley').

The two brothers are both fanatical Manchester City supporters, as are most Mancunians (Man United tend to draw most of their support from outside the city of Manchester itself). Noel's been going to see City since the age of four and admits he was in tears when he first heard their fans taking up *Wonderwall* as a terrace anthem at Maine Road. Guigsy is also a Manchester City fan, Bonehead a Manchester United enthusiast, while Alan White supports Charlton Athletic. Paul Gallagher remembers: 'My Dad started taking me to Maine Road in 1970 and Noel came with us a few years later. We always used to go in at three-quarter time, and me and my kid used to wonder why we couldn't get in from the start. Of course, it was because we couldn't afford it and three-quarter time was when they used to open the Kippax gate to let people out. Me and Noel started going on our own in the late 70s and early 80s, and we were really into it in the glory years of the second division, spending a fortune every week to watch people like Steve Kinsey. Then later on Liam and his mates started going too. We were mad for it then, and went home and away until about '86, when the music really took over.'

Peggy recalls she used to despair at the thought of her sons' future when they were growing up. She recollected the two younger brothers having an early love of music, particularly Noel. 'He was always banging my knitting needles along to The Beatles or the Sex Pistols,' she reflects. 'Liam was obsessed with John Lennon. He bought every Beatles record.'

Tommy also lets slip rather embarrassingly that the two boys shared a love of Alvin Stardust and 'when he came on telly they'd mime along and pretend to be Alvin and I'd catch them singing into hairbrushes and playing air guitar'. He later told *Smash Hits* that both Noel and Liam's original 'wonderwall' was actually the wall of the bedroom they used to share as children in their ex-council house. 'They called it their wonderwall,' he claims. 'It's what they named the single after.' (Noel says he named it after the film *Wonderwall*, which George Harrison scored, in honour of his current girlfriend, Meg Matthews.)

Slick Noel the teenager with two Irish relations.

'In 1983 they both started writing on the wall. Bits of songs, poems, favourite bands, football teams. In one corner Noel wrote "I love Diane Jones" and underneath in the same writing, "Liam is a puff". They'd fight terribly about who had the most writing space. I didn't touch it for years but I wallpapered it before Christmas.'

In 1986 the Gallaghers had their biggest domestic crisis, one which would shape their whole future. After years of tension and during one particular argument, Noel beat up his father when he leapt to his mother's defence. An ambulance had to be called and Tommy was taken to hospital. Peggy immediately left the family home for a nearby council house to start a new life with her three sons. Tommy says: 'I haven't changed the locks, they've still got keys and if they want they can come back.'

The Diane Jones of Noel's youth is described by Tommy as 'one of the nicest, really respectable. I think she caught him with someone else though. Noel was the champ with the girls, he had a good few girlfriends. He used to sneak girls into the house. If I found them misbehaving in the front bedroom, I'd chuck them out. Our Noel usually took girls upstairs, but only because that was where the record player was. He'd play music to them all night, but up until he was 14, Liam used to say "I hate girls, they do my head in.'"

Then, just before the big bust-up at home, Tommy took Liam on a trip to his native village of Duleek. 'He was good at pool, but he was good at the pull, too,' Tommy chuckles. 'All the girls in the village were mad for him. I made a man out of him – he was drinking pints of lager in Big Tom's pub, winning games of pool for a fiver and being a bit of a hit with the birds.'

Tommy also claims that from an early age Liam gained a reputation as a 'mummy's boy'. 'It wasn't Liam's fault,' he points out. 'All the lads round here were Noel's age and all the kids Liam's age were girls. So he'd play with the big lads and he'd come in with a bloody nose, a knock or a cut. When Peggy went out, Liam went with her to keep out of trouble. But he was a tough little kid. A teacher came to our house one day and said she couldn't handle him because he was so lively.'

He adds that there were a lot of tough nuts in Burnage who were a bad influence on Noel and he often caught him playing truant. 'There was a group of lads who robbed a house and I got to know Noel was involved,' he claims. 'He told me he was only doing "look-out", but I made him tell me where the stuff was and then I took it back to the police. He didn't do it again.' It was perhaps that robbery Noel was referring to in an April 1996 interview in *Melody Maker* when in a throwaway line he casually admits to having carried out 'burglaries' when he was younger. That statement consequently caused a furore with Conservative politicians who even managed to persuade Manchester police to investigate its plausibility.

Tommy, who now works as a country and western DJ in Manchester, still has Noel's first guitar. 'I thought if I bought it and put it there, Noel's inquisitiveness would do the rest,' he explains. 'It's Noel's guitar and I'd like him to have it.' Noel learned to play his first Beatles song, *Ticket to ride*, on it at the age of 11. By the age of 13 he was an accomplished guitar player and was even teaching his father to play. Noel claims that when he was 13 or 14 he sent off to John England's catalogue for 'a horrible black acoustic rip-off of a Gibson Hummingbird'. He used to practise *House of the rising sun* and *Ticket to ride* and his earliest hero was Steve Jones, but it was Johnny Marr who first inspired him into wanting to become a full-time musician.

The first proper gig he went to was The Damned at Manchester Apollo in 1980 and one of his favourite shows from years back was The Smiths at the Free Trade Hall around 1984. 'I thought, "I like this band",' he recalls. 'I said to all my mates, "You've got to see this band The Smiths – even if you think they're shit, there's loads of fanny."'

Tommy also kept an old doodle book of Noel's when aged 15, which includes lists of his favourite bands and a large drawing of nuclear bomb mushroom clouds and slogans like 'Why must we destroy this planet?' and 'This whole world is rather huppitytuppity'. He uses the word 'N-O-E-L' to stand for 'No one ever loves'.

Their estranged father still wishes them well, even though his first encounter with them in ten years was a violent confrontation in a Dublin hotel in March 1996. 'They were destined for this,' he says proudly. 'They deserve it. They've done amazingly, more than any dad could ask of his own.'

Peggy also keeps scrapbooks full of Oasis clippings, and pictures of the band litter her walls. 'I used to despair of the boys at times, especially Liam,' she admits. 'I used to go on and on at him to get a proper job. He never did, but he's more than made up for it now.

'Privately, they've got a great admiration for each other. Liam looks up to Noel because of his songwriting ability and Noel looks up to Liam because of his voice. They always look out for each other. It's been a struggle, but they're very close.'

Tommy confesses that he has tried to earn money by telling stories to newspapers about the boys' upbringing but says elsewhere, 'I feel more like a fan than their father. We've been apart for so long it's difficult to feel anything else. I'm proud of them but I'm not going to make any claim on them now that they're famous. I actually try to shy away from being connected with them. People don't believe me, but I don't want to be known as a pop star's dad. I don't go around telling people what my surname is, in case they guess who I am.'

He says that he should have been the band's first manager in their infancy as he knows enough about the music business but now feels he has been shut out completely, even though he'd like to get involved. 'If it wasn't for one silly fight I'd still be there behind them,' he adds. 'There's two sides to every story. I blame Margaret [*Peggy*] for the fight and I blame her for turning the boys against me. They all think I'm some kind of demon. Liam in particular used to worship me. Now he says he hates me, and it's because of what she told them. They all forget I used to take the boys to Ireland every year for a six-week holiday.

Gallagher Neighbourhood Watch Scheme

'You can't always be right, but I think I was a good father and raised the boys the best I could. I'd love to go and see the band playing, but I'm too afraid of the rejection. If I knocked on their dressing-room door I'd get it slammed in my face. That would just be too painful.'

But Peggy, who has refused to speak to Tommy for a decade, is more sceptical of her divorced husband's intentions. 'Their father went out of their lives a long time ago and we've kept it that way,' she says. 'We've had nothing to do with him and we don't want anything to do with him. What does he know about Noel and Liam? I'm surprised he can even remember their names.

'He wouldn't give them any pocket-money, he wouldn't even give them £1 if they needed it. After we split up, he was never there to help them. He was never like a father should have been.' She says the boys stuck close to her and fiercely protected her because 'we're Irish Catholics and we're that kind of family'.

'Liam's a real homebird,' she continues. 'He's got the same friends he's had for years. He loves to come home and go to the pub with his mates. As soon as he gets home the phone just doesn't stop ringing. Liam and I got especially close after his dad left. I always pamper him and we spend a lot of time together. I treat him the way I always have done. He still does my shopping for me and I still tell him off if he deserves it.

'Liam was always a performer and liked to be the centre of things. He always stood out since he was a child and loved to be noticed. I suppose because Noel is a bit older, they don't always get on. Noel is the quieter one. Brothers often argue in families anyway.'

Their older brother Paul could get a job with the Oasis crew at the drop of a hat but feels he wants to furrow his own way in life rather than rely on his brothers' fame. Ironically, it was Paul who was the first Gallagher boy to take up the guitar. He spent a couple of years on just £45 a week on the dole as well as managing a couple of local bands such as Performance, before being appointed Creation's north of England A&R representative in April 1996. He now has his own office and despite Liam's claims that 'we pay your wages', Creation stress they appointed Paul on his own merits.

Noel and Liam left school with no qualifications but Noel got a job with a building firm who were subcontracted to British Gas. One fateful day a giant steel cap fell off a gas pipe the workmen were laying and smashed up Noel's right foot. He was given a cushy job in the stores handing out bolts and wellies and it was in that room that he found time to write songs and strum his guitar. At the age of 20 he began playing at parties and people were amazed he was such a good songwriter.

In 1988 both he and Liam went to see The Stone Roses in Manchester and Noel had a chance meeting with Graham Lambert, the guitarist with Inspiral Carpets. He asked Noel to audition as the new singer with the band. Noel performed The Rolling Stones' *Gimme shelter* and the Inspirals' *Joe*, *Whiskey* and *Keep the circle around* at the audition, which was the night of the Lockerbie disaster. He was turned down, but he was taken on as guitar/technician/roadie and spent two years on the road with the Inspirals. It was this baptism of fire which would pave the way for Noel's own assault on the world of music.

While Noel now has his own pad in London, Liam stays with his Mum whenever he's in Manchester, normally in the same bed and in the same room where he slept as a boy. Both he and Noel used to share the same room while big brother Paul had his own.

Noel describes Peggy as 'a typical Irish mother' and she is the only one who apparently can keep Liam under control. 'On the one hand our Mam's really proud of us,' he told the August 1994 issue of *Vox* magazine. 'She wants to show all the neighbours when we're in the paper. Then she reads it and she's embarrassed. I mean, you can act hard when you're in a band but as soon as we go home, she sits us down at the kitchen table. She tells us we swear too much and says, "So what's this about your sprinkling cocaine on your cornflakes, Noel?" and "Liam, is this true about you going to whorehouses?" There's nothing we can say.' As for Liam's Jack the lad image Noel told the May 1994 issue of the same magazine: '. . . I know that's not really him 'cos as soon as we go home to me Mam's she clips him round the fuckin' ear.'

Tommy Gallagher with Gallagher Granny Ann

The Genesis of Oasis

A young Manchester band called Rain are gigging sporadically around the city in 1991 but usually their sets end in shambles. Their line-up consists of Paul 'Bonehead' Arthurs (born 23 June 1965) on rhythm guitar, Paul 'Guigsy' McGuigan (born 9 May 1971) on bass, and Tony McCarroll on drums. The singer is a guy called Chris Hutton. Guigsy had originally met Bonehead in a pub one night. Bonehead told him he could play the piano and the guitar and that he'd like to form a band. Guigsy couldn't play anything at that stage but Bonehead told him to try bass and initially avoid the top string. Rain mostly did covers, the likes of *Wild thing*. They decided to dispense with Chris. 'Someone said, "Have you ever heard Liam Gallagher singing?", so he came down, had a go and it was "Yes, now we're on it"', Bonehead remembers. The rehearsal took place in the basement of Raffles Hotel.

On 18 August 1991 the band played their first proper gig together as a four-piece at the Boardwalk in Manchester. By now they had changed their name to Oasis, Liam having obtained the idea from a venue called the Swindon Oasis. Oasis supported a local outfit called Sweet Jesus and came on just after The Catchmen. Noel got to hear about his younger brother's fledgling band when he phoned up his mother from Europe while he was on tour with the Inspirals, so among those in the sparse audience were Noel Gallagher and some of Inspiral Carpets. Noel approached Oasis after the gig and they asked him to manage them. He turned them down, but pointed out that he had been writing songs for years and that he'd like to join the band on lead guitar. He insisted he'd be the band's songwriter and they'd have to follow his every instruction. He had learned the ropes of the music world through his stint with the Inspirals and had kept his eyes and ears wide open. During his time with the Inspirals he also struck up a friendship with their monitor engineer, Mark Coyle, who would later produce some of Oasis's earliest work.

They began rehearsing twice a week, and eventually up to six times a week, at the Boardwalk on Little Peter Street, not far from where Noel used to work with the Gas Board. Noel played the band a rough cut of *Live forever*, a song he had written while he was in the storeroom. The others were blown away. They shared the building with other Manchester acts such as The New Fads, D-Tox, Houndogs With a Tumour and Sister Lovers. One early story is that someone posted up a notice on Oasis's door telling them to 'get your own riffs'. The message in fact was directed at The New Fads from D-Tox.

From the spring of 1992 to the summer of 1993 Noel would still roadie with the Inspirals, using spare moments and soundchecks to concentrate on his own material. 'The worst thing was knowing I was miles better than the Inspirals,' he reflects. 'Miles better. But I needed the money [*rumoured to be as much as £500 a week*] and I stuck it out 'cos getting a band off the ground is difficult.'

Oasis played their first gig as a five-piece at the Boardwalk on 19 October, at which they performed four songs. The first number they did was *Columbia*, which was then an instrumental, an acoustic song called *Acoustic song*, a track called *Take me* which Liam and Bonehead wrote, and a popular house tune at the time – they can't remember its name. Around that time they were also rehearsing *Rock 'n' roll star*. 'People were going "Yeah, of course you are, mate, bottom of the bill at the Boardwalk on a fuckin' Tuesday night"', Noel later remembered. 'Pretentious arseholes is what they thought we were. Went down like a knackered life. We thought they were going to be in raptures. And it ended in a bowl of silence. But from that first gig on, I don't know what came over us. We knew we were the greatest band in the world. We'd go, "Fuckin' Happy Mondays, Stone Roses, they haven't got the tunes we've got."'

They were due to record their first demo before Christmas 1991 at the Abraham Moss studios in Cheetham Hill. The tape was obtained by local DJ Pete Mitchell on Key

Oasis at Slane Castle in Ireland in July 1995 with Hollywood actor Johnny Depp.

Liam the showman.

103 but its quality was appalling. Noel would even later deny that he actually played on it. The first track was called *Colour my life* and was likened to local act Northside. The second number was titled *Take me* and had a psychedelic Inspiral Carpets touch to it. Manchester listings magazine *City Life* music editor Chris Sharratt discovered a copy of the tape in the office and reviewed it in the Christmas issue. 'Oasis go for the dramatic build-up here, first acoustic guitar, then pattering drums and bass ... interesting but I'm not too excited,' he wrote. Meanwhile, they played a gig at Dartford polytechnic on 19 April, supporting Revenge and The Ya Yas. The place was full of labourers and Oasis got up their noses so much they were forced to flee the building.

In the summer of 1992, Factory records showed the first sprinkling of interest. The label's head of A&R, Phil Saxe, wanted to put them on a Factory sampler but it never materialised as the company faced bankruptcy. Noel even had a meeting with Factory supremo Tony Wilson, who had launched Joy Division and spearheaded Happy Mondays' 'Madchester' movement. 'He went into a big speech about how the music business and the press was all overrun by cockneys and how baggy had been killed by them all,' Noel later told Radio 1. 'We just said "Right, Tone! Up the workers!" Two weeks later he rang us up and said the tape was too baggy.'

They were now hanging out in Amazon studios and the Inspirals' singer, Clint Boon, was doing his best to help them out. He phoned up Ian Broudie of the Lightning Seeds but nothing came to pass.

Oasis were given their first major feature in the *Manchester Evening News* on 12 June with a piece by Penny Anderson titled 'Just when the music scene is drying up ... the refreshing sounds of Oasis'. Noel described their music as '... not pop, not rock, but somewhere in between, maybe pock? I've always been into guitars,' he added. 'We want to put heavy keyboards on, but keyboard players don't look cool onstage, they just keep their heads down. There has never been a cool keyboard player apart from Elton John.'

Noel claimed that if it had been 1989 they 'would have been signed by now' but 'nobody wants to know so you've got to get to London'. He wisely predicted: 'We're going to bide our time until we feel confident enough to come up and then go for it.'

Oasis had also written *Rock 'n' roll star* at this stage and had passed on a tape to local industry mover Macca, who managed Northside. BBC Radio 5's *Hit The North,* which then had Mark Radcliffe, got Oasis in for a session in the summer of 1992 and they played *Cigarettes and alcohol.* Radcliffe was on holiday so the show was hosted by Mark Riley and New Order's Peter Hook. Liam had a go at Hook and sneered about his leather trousers. Hook told him he would not be welcome at the Hacienda club again and Liam said he was not bothered as it was 'shit' anyway. The recording has since mysteriously disappeared.

Noel had earlier approached Bindi Binning about a gig as Binning was one of the co-ordinators of the inaugural 'In The City', a music festival for unsigned bands which had been started by Factory boss Tony Wilson. Oasis were put on the bill at The Venue on 13 September alongside Machine Gun Feedback, Jealous and Skywalker. The band did not go down too well – Liam's vocals were not up to scratch. Liam and Noel also had a by now normal bickering match onstage. Several A&R representatives were present but most of them thought Oasis sounded too much like The Stone Roses.

The Inspiral Carpets by now had laid off their road crew and Noel realised he would not have a chance to tour with them in America. He was given a 'golden handshake'. He ploughed all his energy into Oasis and approached The Real People's Tony Griffiths about the possibility of recording at their eight-track studio in Liverpool. Noel was surprised when Tony agreed to the request.

Oasis played the Boardwalk again on 22 November, supporting The Cherries and Molly Halfhead. Their set was barely audible, with The Cherries eventually pulling the plug on them – much to the ire of Liam.

Noel next met an old school friend at the Hacienda. They began to discuss The The's *Dusk* album which Noel had just bought. His buddy asked Noel for his demo tape to give to 'our kid'. It turned out he was actually Johnny Marr's brother, Ian. Noel was delighted to hand over an eight-song demo tape to be forwarded to the legendary guitarist. Within 24 hours Johnny rang up Noel and told him he was impressed. They began to talk about vintage guitars and Noel mentioned an instrument shop in Doncaster. They both drove up and Johnny splashed out £9,000 on guitars. He said he'd mention Oasis to his own manager Marcus Russell. The Welshman became interested in Oasis in the early part of 1993 and eventually took them on. No contracts were signed, just a handshake which lasts to this day. The band were hanging out with Liverpool outfit Smaller and they played two gigs together on Merseyside. One of Oasis's covers was Hot Choclate's *You Sexy Thing*. On 31 May Manchester band Sister Lovers were playing at Glasgow's King Tut's Wah Wah's. They were on the bill with 18 Wheeler. Sister Lovers alerted Noel that Creation Records' boss Alan McGee would be at the gig. The Scot had signed the likes of the Jesus and Mary Chain, Primal Scream, The Boo Radleys and My Bloody Valentine. Noel saw it as an opportunity waiting. He later told Irish radio station 2FM: 'So we hired a van, put loads of people in it, charged them money for petrol and told them we'll get you into the gig for free and we'll have a good night and they said fine.

Noel and Bonehead in Dublin (August 1994).

'So we got to the gig after driving all day and the promoter said, "I've never heard of you, you're not supposed to be playing here tonight so we're not going to let you play." So we pointed out the fact that they had only two security guards on the door and there were 17 of us, so I stood there and said, "What are you going to do about that then?" and he said, "Hmm, if you put it like that I can give you half an hour."

'So we went on when the doors opened. It was just about half past seven. Alan McGee was there early and he watched us walk on stage. He asked, "Who's this band?" and someone said, "They're a bunch of guys who threatened to smash the place up if we didn't let them play." He went, "All right, any good?" "Never heard of them, from Manchester, lipping Mancs." He bought a drink, watched the gig, came offstage, gave us a six-album deal. Sounds bizarre, but it's true.'

Debbie Turner, then vocalist with Sister Lovers, says the real story may be slightly different. She says McGee was there with his sister to see one of his bands, 18 Wheeler, but the promoter did not want Oasis to play. 'There were supposed to be four bands playing,' she remembered. 'Us, 18 Wheeler, Boyfriend and Oasis. But when we got there the promoter told us there's no way that other Manchester bands are playing as well. The reason they did play is because we told the promoter that if Oasis didn't, then we wouldn't, and because we were mates with Boyfriend, they said they wouldn't play if we didn't. It didn't actually happen the way it's usually told.'

Alan McGee told BBC Radio 1: 'We heard that this bunch of scallies were going to smash up the club because they had blagged on to play, just like the Sex Pistols. I thought it was funny that somebody was on a Sex Pistols trip or something. Then there were 15 kids from Manchester all sitting around the table and there was one kid in a blue and white Adidas top. He looked amazing, really handsome, looked like Paul Weller. I had no idea that this was Liam Gallagher. I went up the stairs and sure enough this band came on with the front man I had already noticed. He was so confrontational as a frontman that you just thought he'd really got attitude. Then they played the first song and it was really good and I was surprised. The second song happened and it was really good and the guitar solo was outrageous and the guitarist could obviously play. By the third song I had already decided to sign them and then they did *I am the walrus*, an amazing version. Then about ten minutes after they came offstage Noel appeared out of the dressing-room. I just walked up to him and said, "Do you want a record deal?'" McGee phoned up Creation's marketing director, Tim Abbott, early that morning and said he'd just seen 'the new Sex Pistols' and 'the greatest band since The Beatles' who would turn the company around.

Oasis travelled to London and on their first visit to Creation's office they noticed Abbott wearing a Manchester United top. They told him they'd only sign if he removed it. On their second trip Oasis went out with the Creation staff and Noel demanded a chocolate brown Rolls-Royce if they ever became massive. They played a few gigs that summer, supporting Liz Phair and the Milltown brothers and recorded *Columbia* in The Real People's Liverpool studio. It took a few weeks for Oasis to actually sign on the dotted line and during this period they even turned down double what they'd been offered by Creation from the U2-owned Mother Records.

It is now known within the music industry that Oasis were actually signed by Sony records and licensed out to Creation. For the first time I can now reveal the amount they signed for – £60,000, which seems staggering given their worth today

They played their second 'In The City' show in Manchester on 14 September at the Canal Bar but lost out to Blessed Ethel for the award of best new band. Oasis now signed to Sony America's wing Epic and the band played their first London gig at the Powerhaus on 3 November. That week they also signed on Creation's dotted line, but only when McGee acceded to Noel's request to take down a poster of The Farm off his wall.

They played some more dates with The Verve and The Real People and completed their final gig of 1993 at the Krazy House in Liverpool. They then started four days recording in Liverpool's Pink Museum studio. It was there they recorded *Supersonic*, one of the lines of which was inspired by engineer Dave Rott's rottweiler Elsa which had a slight digestive problem and constantly farted!

They left Liverpool and headed for London where they

recorded a Radio 1 *Evening Session* and met up with Primal Scream. While there they recorded *Cigarettes and alcohol*, *Up in the sky*, *Shakermaker* and *Bring it all down*. A white label copy of *Columbia* also created a buzz and got some airplay, Oasis's first national impact on the general public.

Fighting Their Way to the Top

In 1994 Oasis burst on to the indie scene as the most exciting development in British rock in years. Little did they or anybody else know that by the year's end they'd have released the biggest selling debut album in the history of British popular music.

A majestic year starts with the band laid low at the Monnow Valley recording studios in Wales from 7 January with Dave Batchelor (Sensational Alex Harvey Band) producing, but his style does not gel with Noel. As chance (again) would have it, while In Monmouth Noel bumps into one of his all-time heroes, Ian Brown, of The Stone Roses, who is recording a few miles away at Rockfield. Noel is flattered to win Brown's seal of approval. But Creation are not too impressed with the results of 18 days recording, the only tangible end-product being *Slide away*, Noel's favourite track on *Definitely maybe* and the version which finally makes it on the album. There are some Stones covers with Noel singing. The band also shoot the sleeve to *Supersonic* in the Welsh studio. They move to London's Olympic studios to resume recording with Mark Coyle.

On 27 January they play the tiny Splash club in King's Cross. It's an invited-only affair for about 200 people with several hundred more turned away after word of mouth hype, with a one-sided white label copy of *Columbia* being lauded as one of the big finds of recent years. Support is by Cream Soda and among the VIPs present are Reni of the Stone Roses, Mark Lamarr, former Happy Monday Paul Ryder and various members of the Jesus and Mary Chain, the Charlatans, St Etienne, The Boo Radleys and The Verve.

Melody Maker writer Sarra Manning says: 'It's obvious that Oasis are shamelessly plundering 30 years of pop, but come on, who gives a fuck when it sounds so giddy round the gills with adoration?' She predicts: 'They're going to steal your hearts with or without your consent.'

Simon Williams of the *NME* amazingly claims that 'one song sounds exactly like Blur' and concludes that the gig is 'lovely'. He chirps: 'Oasis songs simply roll along with a genuine Up Yours attitude and a lazy beat sufficiently infectious to make gawping, semi-conscious "geezers" of us all, while Liam carelessly chucks melodies on top.'

With the IPC weeklies at King's Reach Tower giving Oasis the thumbs up for their first full London debut, it would only be a matter of time before kudos would turn to world domination. Both Noel and Liam go AWOL for a few days but Noel is reported to have turned up playing drums, if you believe that, with Primal Scream for a live MTV jam while Liam is spotted in Camden market mercilessly teasing the ex-Flowered Up singer.

On 6 February they play a one-off gig in Gleneagles, Scotland, to brush up. Twelve days later, on 18 February, the band are meant to support The Verve at a gig in Amsterdam's Sleepin' Arena Club, their first ever show outside the UK and for some of the band their first time abroad. But needless to say trouble rears its ugly head on the ferry across from Harwich. Liam and Guigsy down a plentiful supply of Jack Daniels and duty free champagne before getting into an argument in the bar. Some of the people they're bickering with are Chelsea supporters while there are also allegations from bar staff that the Oasis duo are passing counterfeit £50 notes. Scuffles with security men ensue before they are both handcuffed and deposited in the brig.

Bonehead wakes to find his room has been ransacked and a lot of gear stolen. He presumes it was a group down the corridor that he had a word or two with earlier on. Tony freaks out and starts banging on all the doors of neighbouring cabins and he and Bonehead are soon detained for causing a disturbance. They join the other two in the detention cell and, once the ship docks, they're put on the next boat home to England. Miraculously, Noel sleeps through the whole drama and finds his band all packed back to Blighty. He makes his way to the club

to tell the management and The Verve that Oasis will have to cancel. 'I'm not around when this sort of thing is going on,' he says later. 'I'm in bed reading the *Independent* with a glass of orange juice.'

On his return to Britain Noel joins the rest of the band to record the album at the Sawmills studios in Golant, Cornwall, where most of the backing tracks are completed in four days with producer and live engineer Mark Coyle. Oasis leave on 4 March to prepare for the *Word*, performing *Supersonic,* their acerbic and punkish debut single to be released on 11 April. The bonus tracks on the 12-inch include *Take me away* and *I will believe*, while the CD version also has *Columbia*, which was previously only available as a white label. The lyrics for *Supersonic* took just half an hour to write and it took eight hours to record and mix in a live set-up with Mark Coyle. *Take me away* was also written the same day and has Noel on vocals.

upcoming tour. Owen Morris is brought in to mix these sessions at Eden and Matrix studios in London, Manchester's Out of the Blue and Loco studios in Wales over the next few months. *Supersonic*, which had already been mixed by Dave Scott, and *Married with children*, recorded in Mark Coyle's living-room with Noel on acoustic guitar, are added. On 18 March they make their first appearance on controversial Channel 4 show *The*

They kick off another short UK tour on 23 March at Bedford Angel (for a reputed standard fee of £100). They retire that night to the Moathouse, where they play a few Beatles numbers in the corridors, upsetting the guests and promptly getting banned. Oasis's sold-out gig with Whiteout at the 100 Club on London's Oxford Road on 24 March sees a broadside in *Melody Maker* with live reviewer Holly Barringer aggressively attacking the 'kids' for latching on to Oasis. 'Oasis are the future, they state with a devilish flourish,' she sneers. "'Bollocks" springs to mind.' She claims *Shakermaker* is a 'mutated version of *I'd like to teach the world to sing*' before ending her vicious onslaught with the observation that 'we'll go and see Oasis and Pulp and Suede and we'll make like we've created some kind of scene that our children will want to know about. The hell they will. This has to end.'

But Keith Cameron of *NME* argues: 'Four rows from the front they sound like the most astute, nay, important signing Alan McGee has made since Ride.' *NME* award *Supersonic* 'single of the week' in its 9 April issue with Cameron enthusing that 'great bands out of Manchester there have been . . . but nothing like this'. He adds, '*Supersonic* is a paragon of pop virtue in a debut single' before rounding off with some questions and answers such as 'Thrilling? Absolutely. Stars? Inevitably. And? Simply a great rock 'n' roll group.'

Surprisingly, *Melody Maker* is more lukewarm in its approach to the debut single from the band they originally 'discovered' through Paul Mathur and championed. Reviewer Peter Paphides says the title track 'comes on my anxiety worries that it's perhaps not a great idea for bands to sound like Blur four years ago. After all, even Blur don't sound like Blur four years ago.' But on the positive side he notes, 'then my lust tells me there's something rather sexy about Liam Gallagher's Ryder-esque drawl and the way he sings'.

Incidentally, one of the lines on *Supersonic* namechecks a 'Mr Sifter' who sold songs to Noel at the age of 16. The 'Mr Sifter' is actually Peter Howard of Sifters record shop in Burnage where Noel used to buy his early Beatles records and where they soon struck up a friendship.

The track enters the UK top 40 singles chart at No 31 and goes straight in at No 1 in the indie charts. Noel would later disclose: '*Supersonic* is about some fucking nine-stone geezer who got Charlie'd off his nut one night . . . it's not about anything. It's just about a feeling, you just get up and play it.' It will be re-recorded towards the end of the year in Liverpool's Pink Museum with Mark Coyle producing for the album version.

While on tour they inevitably get up to bizarre shenanigans again which include being escorted out of Stonehenge after climbing over a fence and being charged with the theft of a fleet of Scottish golf-carts, while Noel punches Liam in the face on stage at a gig in Southampton's Joiners Arms on 29 March and chases him off stage.

They appear in the 'On' section of *NME* on 2 April with the band praising The Stone Roses and Noel pointing out 'for me, punk rock was the Sex Pistols and they were big time fun'. Alan McGee informs the April issue of *Vox* magazine that the music of Oasis is 'a cross between The Kinks, Stone Roses and The Who, and the cover of the tape (their demo tape, which featured early versions of *Columbia*, *Digsy's dinner*, *I will believe*, *Fade away*, *Married with children*, *Bring it on down* and *D'yer wanna be a spaceman*, which is incredibly rare, only ten ever made, is important because it's a Union Jack going down the toilet. That sums up our country at the moment . . . seeing them is what seeing The Stones must have been like in the early days. Brutal, exciting, arrogant.'

The 9 April edition of *Melody Maker* features Oasis in their first major full-page profile in that magazine. 'Listen, right,' says Noel. 'If anybody doesn't buy my music I'm going to be the most upset man in the world. We write music for the guy who walks down the street to get his copy of the fucking *Daily Mirror* and his 20 Bensons every day, and he's got fuck all going for him, he's got no money. Even if somebody can't afford to buy our record, if they put it on the radio while they're cleaning the house, and whistle along and go "fuckin' hell, did you hear that tune?". – That's what it's all about.' He adds: 'Of course we're gonna be compared to the Roses, but even they couldn't write a song like *Digsy's dinner* or *Supersonic*' while Liam chips in 'and we couldn't write a fucking tune like *Fool's gold* or *I wanna be adored*'. Noel predicts an 11-minute epic he has written called *All around the world* will win the Eurovision song contest in two years' time. 'If John Lennon had written this track, he'd have been shot five years earlier,' he argues.

They finish off the tour at the Lomax in Liverpool on 13 April with Pete Wylie, Peter Hooton and The Real

People in attendance. Also there are members of The Farm, who're miffed at recent public put-downs of them by Noel and attempt to present Oasis with a picture of themselves. Farm drummer Roy Boulter vainly waits outside the dressing-room for a confrontation while the picture is deliberately left behind by Oasis (it's later framed by the Lomax owners and placed above the bar).

Their first major *NME* feature appears in the 23 April issue and is now the stuff legends are made of. The interview was conducted by John Harris in a Glaswegian hotel and soon has the Gallagher brothers at each other's throats. After dissing S*M*A*S*H and Miles Hunt, Noel turns his attention to Liam and accuses him of being a 'football hooligan' for getting thrown off the ferry at Amsterdam and suggests that he should go and support West Ham if he wants to act like that. Liam claims that these sort of incidents make him 'proud' and that Noel was 'only gutted 'cos you were in bed, reading your fucking books'.

Noel points out that that's the sort of 'hard' thing the Happy Mondays thrived on but Liam argues that the 'Mondays were not about "we're hard". It was like "we like having loads of Es, being in a band, shagging loads of whores . . ."' Noel: 'No, you like shagging whores.' Liam: 'Yeah, I do. Look, all I've got to say is, I'm having a crack. It's not doing anyone any harm. John Lennon used to do loads of mad things.'

Liam then threatens to assault *NME* writer Johnny Cigarettes for a review which said he was an 'Ian Brown-as-Tim Burgess slob of a frontman'. Liam warns: 'I'll hit him with a bottle, right in the kipper.'

The interview ends with Liam saying of Noel, 'I hate this bastard' and 'I hope one day there's a time when I can smash the fuck out of him. With a fucking Rickenbacker. Right on his nose. And then he can do the same to me.'

Noel explains wearily that these fights happen not only every day, but hourly. 'But it's not hate,' he points out. 'It's love. I don't hate him. I love him. It's one of them. We're brothers, man. It's deep shit.'

Amazingly, the interview is released as a 14-minute long 'record' called *Wibbling rivalry* and reaches number 52 in the singles charts in September 1995 (its cover depicts a picture of the Kray twins, which Reg was apparently not too happy about). Liam later remarks: 'If we had a greengrocer, Gallaghers' greengrocer, we'd argue over which way to set out the apples and the pears.'

On 29 April Oasis headline another UK tour, kicking

off at Hull's Adelphi and concluding on 14 May at the Leadmill in Sheffield. Almost all the gigs are sold out. The London New Cross show on Friday, 13 May seems like a recipe for disaster with Oasis sharing the bill with Shed Seven and Cast, while a number of celebrities who're not exactly flavour of the month with Noel turn out, including Suede's Simon Gilbert and now departed member Bernard Butler and Ride's Andy Bell among others. Fortunately, there are no major incidents, although Shed Seven did find their drum kit removed by Oasis from the centre stage and Liam threatening to remove some banners. Liam later conks out in the London rock 'n' roll hotel, The Columbia, and, busily engaged with the sound of groaning emanating from his room, colourfully turns down the Shed's drummer Alan Leach's suggestion of having a late drink after Leach went to the trouble of climbing on to Liam's balcony!

During their London sojourn they're persuaded by the Boo Radleys to go to Blur's home stomping ground of the Good Mixer in Camden Town. There follows an altercation with Graham Coxon in the toilets and the chant 'Blur are cockney c**ts'. After complaints they are barred from the pub. This will be a taste of things to come over the next couple of years. The latest Oasis tour bus song goes to the tune of the Small Faces' *Lazy Sunday*: 'Wouldn't it be nice to be a fucking cockney/wouldn't it be nice to be in fucking Blur/what a c***'. On to the Camden Underworld where Oasis get into a ruck with some crusties and are turfed out.

A noticeable rift emerges between Tony McCarroll and the rest of the band over the coming weeks, with incidents cropping up such as at football matches where the others would refuse to pass Tony the ball.

Oasis's debut *Vox* interview appears in the 'coming attractions' section of the May issue. 'I remember The Stone Roses selling out clubs and thousands of people being turned away,' Noel recalls. 'Then it dawned on me, I'd written that song, mate, five years ago and better than that. Then the club thing happened and I got side-tracked. I just wanted to go out, take lots of drugs and dance around all night. After that finished, the band got together and I started writing songs.'

The May edition of *Select* magazine gives away a compilation tape which includes a version of *Fade away*. Noel explains: 'It's about when your teachers ask you what you want to be when you grow up. No one ever says, "I wanna make tea for factory workers." You always say, "I wanna be a spaceman or a fireman or a pop star." As you get older and more cynical, you find out the world is a bag of fuckin' shit, and the dreams you had as a child fade away. You end up doing whatever you've got to do to get by, which is basically fucking washing dishes in restaurants.'

A third headline tour runs from 1 to 12 June. On 3 June Bonehead is forced to fork out £145 to the Forte hotel in Cardiff, having trashed his room the previous night. 'It was a real sexual rush I got,' he later explains, with the manageress complaining, 'These rock 'n' roll bands, they're always trouble.' That evening at Ilford Island they're presented with dozens of pairs of trainers, at £30 a go, by Bedford promoter Neil Primmett. But the gig is ruined by stagedivers and Liam is left shaken afterwards.

They make an acoustic appearance at Creation's 'Underdrugged' night at the Royal Albert Hall on 4 June alongside Ride, Bob Mould and The Boo Radleys. Liam cries off that night with 'a sore throat'. Noel and Bonehead perform *Forever young*, *Shakermaker* and *Whatever* while Liam suddenly recovers his voice to bombard them with abuse from one of the VIP boxes.

The 4 June issue of *NME* finally sees them landing their first cover story in that paper. Liam is pictured on his own outside 'The Oasis Bar' (taken at the King's hotel in Newport) with the heading: 'Totally Cool. Oasis: What the world is waiting for'. Writer Simon Williams depicts a hotel from hell scene after their gig in Portsmouth's Wedgewood Rooms. He describes Liam and Noel having a fist fight 'about an ex-girlfriend, allegedly'. Guigsy tries to break the fight up but gets two thumps. Bonehead is in the swimming pool next to the bar but soon chairs are flying through a plate-glass window and landing in the water.

'It's a stupid place to put a pool, innit?' Liam contends the next morning. 'It was just asking for trouble putting us in this hotel.'

Noel agrees: 'Those plate-glass windows are just saying, "Throw a chair through me!'" Noel also tells Williams that music for him at the moment is dead. 'It's poncey and serious and everyone's gotta make some sort of statement,' he opines, 'whether it be about *Parklife* or their feminine side or their politics. But we're just a rock 'n' roll band – we say all you need is cigarettes and alcohol. Everyone's dead into analysing, but don't analyse our band. "That's a good one, that is. What does it mean?" Who gives a fuck what it means?'

Williams's journey with the band also brings him on a motorway ride from Newport to Derby with Bonehead at the steering-wheel of their trusted van. Only Bonehead starts to dive into the back in a traffic jam. Williams describes them as 'the muppet babies, a danger only unto themselves'.

Noel explains that Liam is always winding him up and he normally points out to his kid brother, 'Shut up you fucking dick, I used to change your fucking nappies.' He adds: 'Basically, if he's asking for a smack in the mouth he'll get one. And the same applies to me – if I'm asking for a smack in the mouth, I'll get one.'

They spend more time in Monnow Valley studios, completing the recording of the debut album. Some songs are reputed to have been mixed over 100 times. They meet up with Ian Brown again. *Shakermaker* is released on 20 June. The seven-inch and cassette version is backed by *D'yer wanna be a spaceman*? (with Noel on vocals). The 12-inch adds *Alive* (demo) while the CD version includes all those tracks plus a live version of *Bring it on down*. It is awarded 'single of the week' in *NME* by Mark Sutherland, who says 'you know you're dealing with greatness'. Initially, the band intimate they won't remove the line 'I'd like to buy the world a coke' from *Shakermaker*, added to the New Seekers' style line already in it, 'I'd like to teach the world to sing'. Creation see red and envisage the Coca-Cola people in Atlanta looking for royalties. At first Noel shows some bravado: 'We might have to write off half the fucking royalties, but fuck it. For someone in a suit to come along and say we've got to change a song we've been playing for two years isn't on. If we ever get to pay back our advance, which most bands don't, then it's just going to be another five grand on top.' Despite Noel's protestations the track is eventually released with the change: 'I'd like to be somebody else.'

The band are presented with the first vinyl test pressings of *Definitely maybe*. But the songs are so long and the grooves so close together that they feel the sound isn't powerful enough so they decide to cut the LP on two 12-inch discs instead and add in an extra track. Noel immediately gets down to writing *Sad song*.

On 22 June they re-record *Live forever*, *Sad song*, *Whatever* and *I am the walrus* for Radio 1's *Evening Session*. The next evening Noel joins Billy Talbot and Ralph Molina of Neil Young's legendary band Crazy Horse onstage at London's King's College, where they had been performing with Ian McNabb. Crazy Horse had visited Manchester to see Oasis and were insistent that Noel join them onstage in London. They perform versions of Echo and the Bunnymen's *Rescue* and *Sly Saxon* and the Seeds' *Pushin' too hard* with Noel taking guitar solo. He later gushes: 'My Mum's dead proud of me. I've had my picture taken with Arthur Lee. I've been on stage with Crazy Horse and I'm going to have my picture taken with Johnny Cash. All I need now is to get my picture taken with Burt Bacharach and I've got the full set.'

On the afternoon of Sunday 26 June, they make their debut at Glastonbury on the *NME* stage (Blur headline that evening). They're slotted in between Echobelly and Credit to the Nation. Noel almost misses the gig as he watches some naked didgeridoo players in the Green field. He soon gets his act together when a fan tells him that Oasis are on next.

'Are you gonna wake up then for some real songs?' goads Liam upon taking the stage. They perform nine songs, including the habitual encore *I am the walrus* to an ecstatic reception. Afterwards, they retire to the Inspiral Carpets' tour bus for a party and when the Inspirals eventually turn up Noel asks incredulously, 'What are you doing in here?' *Select* review the gig as follows: 'Any band that has a song called *Cigarettes and alcohol* must be good (and maybe a little peaky at times). Oasis are a Big Thing now, reportedly, and thus the field is packed with well-wishers and girls who must make moist contact . . .'

It describes the 'best bit' as 'Liam standing rigid at the bits when he didn't have to sing, looking like a complete lunatic. Ha, ha.' That particular festival hits the news when five fans are shot and injured on Saturday evening by a man with a pistol in a drugs-related incident.

Shakermaker enters the charts at No 11 on 27 June and on 30 June they make their debut appearance on *Top of the Pops*. Next Oasis take off for the New Music Seminar in New York. My first and only time at that particular music extravaganza was in 1991 and I found it to be a more rap-orientated, back-slapping, exhibition-style trade fair with a few sideshow gigs as showcases. Oasis would make their American debut at the Wetlands club on 21 July sandwiched between foreign acts Lotion and X-CNN. Other British bands to play the NMS include Echobelly, The Orb and S*M*A*S*H.

Oasis open their New York debut with *Shakermaker*. One punter is not amused when he shouts in an English accent, 'Dance, you bastards.' 'Oasis may be as exciting to watch as goldfish, but if you close your eyes and use your imagination they're more prime than Primal Scream,' says *Melody Maker* reviewer Jon Wiederhorn, who predicts 'pretty soon we'll be eating out of their dry, dirty palms'. The following day whilst in New York they shoot the video for their next single, *Live forever*, in Central Park but as ever a fight breaks out. Liam becomes infuriated when Noel – allegedly – claims that his little brother had wet his bed the night before! Tension had already built as Liam wanted to turn the event into an unscheduled gig by hiring a PA but Noel refuses. 'Elvis Presley doesn't want to do it,' Liam sneers. 'That's why he's a c*** and I hate him.' Liam throws a half-eaten burger at Noel. Meanwhile they also pay homage to John Lennon by visiting the Strawberry Fields memorial garden in Central Park and the Dakota building where the Beatles star was shot in 1980.

On their return to London they book into The Columbia Hotel. A normal night smashing the place up ensues but the straw which breaks the camel's back is Bonehead throwing a television out the window, which lands through the front window of the manager of the hotel's Mercedes. Liam recalls: 'There was a lot of pot going around and we'd got some pipes. We were drinking as well and in the end we just trashed it.' Columbia director Michael Rose says: 'I can't remember the last occasion when someone was banned. We wouldn't bar a band unless we feel we have justifi-

able reason.' They have the distinction of joining The Fall and The Mission of being the only bands to be barred from The Columbia, the rock 'n' roll hotel in London.

In a rare feat Oasis grace the covers of both *Melody Maker* and *NME* in their 6 August issues. *Melody Maker* feature them with the slogan 'Oasis: supersonic in the USA', while Liam and Noel don the cover of *NME* in a special on British bands at the NMS entitled 'Scary tale of New York'.

When provoked by an American fan in a hotel lobby about the merits of Pearl Jam and Nirvana, Liam storms: 'Don't talk to me about Nirvana. He was a sad c*** who couldn't handle the fame. We're stronger than that. And you can fuck your fucking Pearl Jam.' The incident is witnessed by *Melody Maker's* Paul Mathur who also reports Noel's passion for early Bee Gees material but distaste for The Clash and The Beach Boys. 'Until six months ago I thought Blondie were French,' he adds. 'I think we'll be the most important band in the fucking world,' Liam tells *NME*. 'If time is on our side and there's not much bad shit and none of us dies, then we'll be the new Beatles. We'll mean just as much . . .

'If the band split up, I wouldn't stop, I'd go on. I wouldn't just be a singer. I'd carry on as a guitarist/singer just like Lennon. I love him, I love his spirit, I love it all. I'll never meet him, but I'm as close as could be, just because I'm totally into what he was all about . . . John Lennon is living now, living out there, living in everybody who's into the Beatles. He's living in me – simple as that.'

NME award Public Enemy's *Give it up* 'single of the week' in the same issue with reviewer John Mulvey comparing *Live forever* to The Real People 'though much, much better'. He then says it's similar to The La's *There she goes* or even The Stone Roses's *Made of stone*. 'A terrific record,' he concludes.

They play the inaugural T in the Park festival in Glasgow, where they kick footballs into the crowd. On 8 August *Live forever* is released. In another Beatles coincidence it was released 25 years to the day since the famous 'Abbey Road' photoshoot. On 15 August it rockets into the UK top 40 at No 10.

Apparently, the cover shot on *Live forever* is the house in Melrose Avenue in Liverpool belonging to Aunt Mimi and Uncle George – where Oasis's hero John Lennon grew up. The single is backed by an acoustic version of *Up in the sky* with Noel on vocals, *Cloudburst* and a live version of *Supersonic* from April. It charts at No 10 with Noel later wondering why a song like it did not go to No 1 compared to the likes of *Some might say*.

Noel discloses to the August issue of *Vox* that he has been evicted from his London flat and has spent the past three weeks sleeping on friends' sofas, including Johnny Marr's. 'Creation doesn't pay us enough money,' he moans. 'That's why I got kicked out of my flat. Last Sunday was my 27th birthday and do you know how I spent it? In bed, in a tiny hotel room, on my own with the phone off the hook. No wonder I'm depressed.' As to their reputation: 'If we're the wildest fuckin' rock 'n' roll band in the country, then British music must be in a pretty sorry state.'

Liam agrees: 'We're definitely not the bunch of twats we're made out to be. People can say what they want about Oasis, but we all know that we're not constant 24-hours-of-the-fuckin'-day hooligans.' Yes, Liam, you do have to get some sleep sometimes!

Controversy again hits Oasis on the second night of the tour on 9 August at Newcastle's Riverside Centre, where Noel says there had been a really good atmosphere until a lout, wearing a large ring, made his way up the front. 'We were halfway through the fourth song called *Bring it all down*,' Noel tells Irish DJ Dave Fanning on his 2FM show. 'I was doing the guitar solo, and it does excite a bit of energy in the crowd, and I was sort of playing away and this guy jumped up on stage and he just hit me in the eye and cut it open. Then I batted him with the guitar and we jumped into the crowd and the crowd jumped on us.'

The band scarpered back onstage and took refuge in the dressing-room. But more aggro followed: 'The tour bus was surrounded by 300 people and it got smashed up. Some of the equipment was damaged, we got damaged. But ironically enough on the whole tour that was where we sold the most T-shirts! It was pretty scary when it was happening but we can laugh about it now because we're here and we're in one piece.'

The riot had been inflamed by Newcastle fans pouring scorn on Manchester City, although Noel weirdly admits that the strobes at the gig could have also made blood boil. In a rare sign of fraternity, Liam later reveals to BBC Radio 1 that he came to the rescue of Noel: 'When somebody does that you don't think of being a pop star or being in a band or the people in the audience. We're here to play songs, we're not about fighting. We do the songs, do the set, get off, splendid evening had by all.'

Noel adds: 'People have said to us, "John Lennon would have gone back on." No, he wouldn't have. Music is the be all and the fans of the band are the be all and end of it all, but I've only got two eyes. If one goes I don't get another one back. At the end of the day it's only rock 'n' roll and I'm not prepared to donate parts of my body to the cause.'

On their escape the Oasis tour bus crashes into a VW Golf belonging to 22-year-old toolmaster Neil Spencer. But it makes a getaway to bring Noel to Newcastle's Royal Victoria Hospital. The next day Noel phones Johnny Marr up from his Leeds hotel and rather embarrassingly confesses that his beloved Gibson Les Paul Sunburst is in bad need of repairing, having been smashed over a Geordie's tough skull. A couple of hours later a taxi pulls up to the hotel with a new Les Paul sent by Johnny. It is accompanied by a note which reads, 'You'll like this one, it's a lot heavier and will fracture anybody's skull if you get a good swing at it.'

Therapy? Andy Cairns reviews *Live forever* in the 13 August edition of *Melody Maker*. 'I started off quite liking it until the Eric Clapton *Wonderful tonight* guitar solo comes in at the end,' he says. 'Music for old bastards.'

On 14 August Oasis, along with a number of other British bands such as The Verve and Primal Scream perform at the Hultsfred festival in Sweden. Liam twists his ankle when he jumps off the tour bus (he had earlier climbed on top of it and draped a Union Jack around him as he dodged power lines while the bus meandered its way through the festival site). As he hobbles into the hotel he recalls 'walking along and this chair comes flying past me, then another, then another. I thought it's going to be a good night!'

Bobby Gillespie and the Primals are staying in the same hotel but wisely check out in the early hours as Oasis and The Verve go on the rampage when the hotel management try to close the bar. They throw telephones through windows and generally smash the place up. They are forced to pay £800 to the hotel manager before all and sundry are arrested, escorted to the nearest ferry port and deported from Sweden. The usually reserved Swedish press go crazy and in much the same way they branded English fans as football hooligans at the European Championships in 1992 as 'English scum', Oasis are given similar front-page 'accolades' on the national *Skol Albino Gazette*.

The Forum in London on Monday 16 August, would be Oasis's biggest British show to date, with the Astoria also sold out the following night. The Forum was once lovingly known as the Town and Country Club and consistently topped the music weeklies' poll for best venue. After the 2,000-strong sold out Forum gig Paul Weller walks into the dressing-room and has a mock argument with Noel. The two had met for the first time at the summer's Glastonbury festival. Weller tells him that they were good but they should do encores. Noel says he enjoyed *Wildwood* but Oasis would better it. He then tells him jokingly to get out of the room and 'Tell me I'm God'. No doubt some people already believe Noel is one without him telling them.

On the Wednesday evening they're ensconced yet again in the *Top of the Pops* studios at Elstree where Liam is still nursing his wounded foot. Also recording that night is sensual New York singer Sophie B. Hawkins, a resurrected China Black and American R 'n' B stars Boyz II Men. Noel turns on his usual tongue-in-cheek charm to Sophie when she comes over to say hello. He asks her what the B in her name stands for. 'Ballantyne,' she replies. Noel coyly asks does that mean 'you always ring the bell on time?' When she tells them she's from Manhattan he quips, 'Man, hat an' what? That's what I wanna know.' Sophie B. asks: 'Are you guys stoned already?'

They play another sold-out show at London's Astoria the next night with their *Top of the Pops* broadcast going

out earlier in the evening. Evan Dando of the Lemonheads turns up at the aftershow party in the Leisure Lounge and berates Liam for saying earlier in the year that 'Kurt Cobain was a sad c*** who couldn't handle fame'.

The 20 August edition of *Melody Maker* sees reviewer Simon Price tear into Oasis after a gig at Leeds's Irish Centre. He says: 'Oasis have hitched a ride on the southern bourgeoisie's patronising, romanticised adoration of straight talking northerners.' He claims their songs recycle the likes of Wham's *Freedom* (!), T Rex's *20th century boy,* Creedence Clearwater Revival's *Proud Mary* and The Sex Pistols' *Pretty vacant* and of course he drags up the New Seekers comparison with *Shakermaker* while pointing out 'most of their lyrics suck'. The magazine's little backlash is offset by awarding *Live forever* 'single of the week' in the same issue with Sarra Manning describing it as 'this brilliant piece of, well, brilliance'.

Further dates in Holland and the UK follow but there are thankfully no more bruising incidents.

Definitely Maybe a Great Year

The band prepare to release *Definitely maybe* and I finally have my first face-to-face encounter with Noel and Bonehead in Dublin's Conrad Hotel. They seem pretty laid back and convivial as they relax in a sunsoaked conservatory. They are excited about the impending release of the album. I tell them I listened to it a couple of days beforehand on a train journey to Belfast and was highly impressed. They want to know about the 'situation' in Belfast (Guigsy's father is from there and he spent much of his holidays when he was young on the Falls Road). But one thing that comes across quite strongly, and which surprises me, is their snide attitude and total disregard for Tony McCarroll. But we part on good terms.

They release *Live by the sea* on 28 August, recorded in Southend in April, and the tracklisting is: *Rock 'n' roll star, Columbia, Digsy's dinner, Some might say, Acquiesce, Headshrinker, Good to be free, Cigarettes and alcohol, Married with children, Sad song, D'yer wanna be a spaceman, Talk tonight, Slide away, Supersonic, I am the walrus.* On 30 August they release *Definitely maybe*. The full CD and tape tracklisting is: *Rock 'n' roll star, Shakermaker, Live forever, Up in the sky, Columbia, Supersonic, Bring it all down, Cigarettes and alcohol, Digsy's dinner, Slide away* and *Married with children*. The vinyl version has one bonus track, *Sad song*. Alan McGee describes it as 'the best British album of the last ten years. Not only that, it will be to 1994 what *Never mind the bollocks* was to 1977 and *Nevermind* was to 1991.'

Noel says that the reason *Rock 'n' roll star* is the first track is because lyrically it sets up the album for what's to come. He wrote it after watching The Rolling Stones doing *Brown sugar* on *Sounds of the Seventies* and it reminded him of being a kid and wanting to be a rock 'n' roll star. *Shakermaker* is more of a rip-off of The Beatles' *Flying* than anything else, he admits, but he insists it has no connection with The New Seekers' *I'd like to teach the world to sing*. He says the song is full of characters from his childhood. He explains *'Mr Clean'* is from the Jam's song; *'Mr Ben'* is from the *Mr Ben* TV series; *'Mr Soft'* is from the softmints commercial, about the character who walks down the street and bumps into soft lamp-posts; 'Mr Sifter' has already been explained. *Live forever*, he adds, is about a friend who could be your friend for life and the way he looks at their good points rather than their bad points.

Up in the sky is a warning to young people not to look up to figureheads or 'the voice of a generation'. *Columbia* is 'our little nod to dance music', while he admits the lyrics to *Supersonic* mean absolutely nothing and he describes it as their *I am the walrus*. He adds that there was a tin of Alka Seltzer in the cupboard of the studio they were recording in and the engineer's dog was a rottweiler called Elsa. He acknowledges that the riff to *Cigarettes and alcohol* is obviously T-Rex but adds 'it's a youth anthem about basically having a bottle of beer and a packet of cigarettes.'

Digsy's dinner is about the singer of Liverpool band Smaller, Digsy Deasy. One day Digsy asked Noel around to his house for lasagne and Noel thought it was so funny he'd put it into a song. *Slide away* is a love song about someone whose identity he refuses to reveal but he says she knows who she is and observers guess it's probably his previous girlfriend of six years (Louise Jones, who works for Manchester-based promoters SJM. She would tell '*The Sun*', 'I don't want to belittle our relationship. The time we lived together was very special but that chapter's over for both of us.'

Married with children is inspired by an incident one night when he was watching the American comedy of the same name on late-night TV and being scowled at by Louise, with him eventually comparing himself to the TV character Al Bundy. He disclosed that the song is about pettiness in a relationship. The vinyl version of the album contains *Sad song*, which he says was a last-minute addi-

tion and meant to be a sad, defeatist song. On first hearing it Alan McGee burst into tears.

The front sleeve of the album feature's Bonehead's living-room in his three-storey house in Manchester. The sleeve is designed by Brian Cannon, who arranges all the singles' sleeves too. Cannon admits he got the idea for the album sleeve from the back of The Beatles' *Oldies but goldies*, which depicts the Liverpool band caught by surprise in a Japanese dressing-room. The Oasis sleeve features a picture of singer Burt Bacharach belonging to Noel in the bottom left corner, and the footballer in the blue shirt in the fireplace is legendary 70s Manchester City player Rodney Marsh. Some fans have mistaken him for George Best, but Georgie, even though he's a former Manchester United player, can be seen in a picture in the window because Oasis consider him a top geezer! The TV features a freeze frame of a man's face being squeezed in *The Good, the Bad and the Ugly*, one of the band's favourite films. The globe comes from producer Mark Coyle's house and was spun and thrown in the shot while the mirror on the wall reflects Bonehead's garden. Believe it or not the red liquid in the wine glass is actually Ribena! The close-up shot of Noel on the inside pull-out sleeve is the only one he likes of himself and he says he normally wears sunglasses because he's always out of it. The scooter belongs to Liam, but he can't actually ride it and it usually sits outside his mum's house. The first pressings of the CD were in black with the millions of others in blue and Noel is annoyed that he gave all his black ones away before he realised they'd become collectors' items.

The album was recorded twice, some parts thrice, and mixed several times. It had taken seven months to record in seven different studios and cost what now seems a measly £75,000. Noel says later: 'I hope this album inspires somebody to get off their arse and form a fucking band. We just feel so isolated at the moment. If we're The Beatles, where's The Rolling Stones? Where's The Who and The Kinks?'

Melody Maker's 27 August edition gives *Definitely maybe* a 'bloody essential' billing in its star rating system. Reviewer Paul Lester says: '*Definitely maybe* is what the world's been waiting for, a record full of songs to live to, made by a gang of reckless northern reprobates (yeah, we hacks love a bit of rough) who you can easily dream of joining.'

Sean O'Hagan says in *The Face*: 'Suspect production doesn't stop this being an LP of classic pop singles (spot the borrowed riffs) . . . Stone Roses, where are you?'

NME award the album an impressive nine out of ten and a cartoon accompanying the review by Ted Kessler depicts Noel and Liam boxing each other. 'With *Definitely maybe* Oasis have encapsulated the most triumphant feeling, it's like opening the bedroom door one morning and discovering some fucker's built the Taj Mahal in your back garden and then filled it up with your favourite flavour of angel delight.'

During their stayover in London they shoot the video for *Cigarettes and alcohol* in front of a select gathering at The Borderline Club and it turns into a full-blown gig at which they perform a new song, *Listen up*, which will later be a B-side. On 30 August Oasis are joined by Evan Dando again for an impromptu 'unplugged' gig at London's Virgin Marble Arch megastore to launch *Definitely maybe*. Only 200 people are let in even though 1,200 queued up for six hours, but the rest of the fans eventually manage to get albums signed. Liam hands Evan a tambourine which he rattles for the duration of the gig, occasionally joining in on backing vocals. The set includes *Shakermaker, Supersonic, Live forever, Slide away* and *Sad song*. They also premiere *Whatever*.

'We met about six months ago and hit if off,' Dando says of his relationship with Noel. 'Then last night, we collided in Paris. We'd both been playing the Lowlands festival in Holland this weekend and we wrote a song together called *Purple parallelogram*. I really like Oasis's lack of pretensions.' The next day Oasis play a gig in Buckley, Wales, with Dando providing a five-song slot along with playing tambourine in Oasis's set..

On 2 September Oasis arrive in Stockholm to play a show at the Gino club. On his way into rehearsals Noel spots an altercation in the building opposite. He doesn't believe some Swedish fans' explanation that a man had just committed suicide by jumping out of a window because he couldn't get a ticket for the Oasis gig (this has never been substantiated). The Swedes had gone crazy about Oasis and *Definitely maybe* was released a whole week before it was in the UK and went straight into the Swedish charts at No 4, selling 20,000 copies in the process. The same Swedish paper which earlier denounced them as 'English scum' now heralds their return with a centre-page spread titled 'They're back!'

Oasis play their first-ever Irish show on 3 September in Dublin's Tivoli, having caught a 6 a.m. flight from Stockholm to London and a connection to Dublin. The 1,000-capacity venue is jammed to the rafters and Oasis have created the same buzz in town as when Suede first played here the previous year. Blur also played the Tivoli on their second trip to Dublin, having performed at the much smaller McGonagle's in the spring of 1991.

It's pointless trying to brave the tiny backstage area where Oasis are holed up with half their families. Evan again shows up. Strangely, some friends spot him walking down a street outside on his own an hour after the gig, enquiring if they know any hotels which are still open. He obviously forgot, or was unaware, that Oasis are staying in the Green Isle Hotel, six miles outside the city in what can only be described as an industrial estate. Evan reputedly smashes in a TV set that night and is so embarrassed that he put the contents into a suitcase only for customs officials to stop him at Heathrow airport in London and ask what the hell he is up to!

Liam and Guigsy also have an unusual encounter at Heathrow. While looking at a guitar magazine with Pete Townsend on the cover in the lounge, they spot the former The Who guitarist in person across the room reading *The Face* with Oasis on the cover. Both parties make themselves known to each other amid much backslapping.

Oasis's hotel in Dublin is reported to have survived their visit, which struck me as odd – several months later when myself and a friend gatecrashed the same place with Cast, we were met by a conceited little porter who wanted us to produce our room keys. We later learned from Cast's press officer, who was in our company but just visiting the hotel like us, that the porter's main reason for flipping out was that he took umbrage at her presence and insinuated that Cast were using her as a bit on the side! The porter threatened to call the police if we didn't leave. 'Call the police if you want,' roared Cast as they enticed us upstairs, where we eventually persuaded room service to bring up some beer.

Oasis head on to Belfast the next evening and learn they've gone straight to No 1 in the album charts with the fastest selling debut by a British band in the 90s, shifting a phenomenal 150,000 units in just one week. It even beats off stiff competition and a £2 million TV ad campaign by the Three Tenors (Domingo/Carreras/Pavarotti) for the coveted top spot. But a Creation spokesman is nonplussed when he remarks, 'The fact that the Three Tenors decide to release their album at the same time means nothing to us. After all, it's just three fat blokes shouting.' The album is Creation's first ever No 1, the nearest contenders for top album in the past being Primal Scream's *Give out but don't give up* (No 2) and Sugar's *Beaster* (No 3).

Oasis return to Manchester for a homecoming gig at the Hacienda on 5 September. Turning up for the gig are the usual friends and families plus Shaun Ryder, New Order's Peter Hook, Johnny Marr, Digsy of Smaller and, of course, Evan Dando. Oasis kick off with *Columbia* and roll through *Bring it on down*, *Up in the sky, Digsy's dinner, Shakermaker, Live forever, Supersonic, Cigarettes and alcohol, Slide away* and finally *I am the walrus.*

Within two weeks of its announcement seven of the ten UK dates on the forthcoming tour starting on 30 November sell out, including London's Hammersmith Palais and Manchester's Academy. An extra date in Brighton is added due to demand. On 12 September Oasis head off for a six-show tour of Japan, and their first gigs in the land of the rising sun. At 7 a.m. they're still in Maida Vale having partied the night away with Primal Scream at Scream manager Alex Nightingale's house. Liam and Noel are so rowdy on the flight that an exasperated air hostess upgrades them to the first-class where there are fewer passengers to annoy. Nice one, if you can get away with it!

There are girls waiting at Tokyo airport, at the hotel,

at the Quatro venue. Some of the girls wear Manchester City shirts and the band are bombarded with presents, from obscure Beatles bootlegs to Noel being handed a £500 black double-breasted Jean-Paul Gaultier jacket.

The last night in Tokyo is Oasis's 100th gig and afterwards they go to the Poppongi's Cavern Club where a Beatles cover band, The Parrots, are performing. Noel asks them to support Oasis on their next Japanese tour and is dragged up to play *Hey, you've got to hide your love away*. Oasis take the bullet train to Nagoya the next day where for the first time ever they do an encore (*Rock 'n' roll star*). Guigsy sums up their lifestyle: 'I can't stand these groups who whine on about how tough life on the road is. We love it – and we go for it.'

Noel gives the 17 September issue of *Melody Maker* a list of songs and albums which changed his life. They are: The Beatles' *The red album*/*The blue album*; The Jam's *Snap*; The Sex Pistols' *Never mind the bollocks*; The Who's *I can see for miles*/*Anyway anyhow anywhere*; Burt Bacharach's *This guy's in love with you*; The Bee Gees' *To love somebody*; The Smiths' *How soon is now*; The Stone Roses' *She bangs the drums*; The La's' *There she goes*; Neil Young and Crazy Horse's *Weld*; The Kinks' *Greatest hits*; Blondie's *Hanging on the telephone*; The Small Faces' *Greatest hits*; The Faces' *Stay with me*. As for his reverence to Bacharach he says: 'How can something this simple be beyond so many people? If you can take a girl home and listen to this record and can't get a shag there must be something wrong with you.' He adds he played *This guy's in love with you* to Bobbie Gillespie when the Scream's singer asked him to play his favourite song. Gillespie was so impressed that 'we've been best mates since'.

On 20 September they take a direct overnight flight from Tokyo to Seattle. It's Liam's 23rd birthday on the 21st, and for one partial to celebrating he gets to salute his birthday twice flying through two time zones. *Definitely maybe* has already shifted 60,000 copies in the US and all five shows on the west coast are sold out.

Oasis and Blur accidentally bump into each other at San Francisco's Live 105 radio station. The two bands meet in the hospitality room with Oasis due to go on air with DJ Steve Masters. First words from Damon to Liam:

'All right, geezer?' First words from Liam to Damon: 'Nish, wanker!' But relations are fairly cordial as Masters brings Blur into the studio just after Oasis finish playing *Supersonic* live. Liam asks in an American accent for the Blur song *The debt collector* to be played and is granted his request. Most of the phone calls are for Blur. Damon and his band go to the Bottom of the Hill club that night to see Oasis in action.

On 28 September Oasis do a phone-in with fans on Los Angeles radio station KROQ. Liam loses his temper when some callers go on about scooters and the like. 'Look, we're not fuckin' mods, alright,' he scowls. Another fan asks Noel if he ever considered a penis extension. Noel tellingly replies that Oasis already have one on drums and wouldn't recommend it. They're pulled off the air by an irate DJ. Later that evening they're thrown out of Johnny Depp's Viper club, where River Phoenix died, after a fracas with some bouncers at closing time. They then head for Bonehead's brother's house a few blocks away. Bonehead sets up some equipment, plays *Supersonic* over and over again until six LAPD cars arrive and caution him about disturbing the peace.

The next day they play Los Angeles's legendary Whiskey-A-Go-Go club. Ringo Starr is spotted there with his wife. The bass amp blows up during the first song, *Rock 'n' roll star*. They play it again. A fan dives onstage, with Liam warning the audience not to encroach on 'his' stage. Noel insists on singing harmony to parts of Liam's vocals and a cameraman keeps on getting in Liam's way. Things begin to hot up for him with the brothers eventually squaring up to each other at the end of *Shakermaker*, midway through the set. Liam cuffs Noel with a tambourine round the back of his head. They continue bickering and Liam walks offstage, refusing to join in the customary last song, *I am the walrus*. The band stay locked in the dressing-room for over an hour afterwards with Liam finally storming off down Sunset Boulevard on his own with a towel draped over his shoulders.

News reaches home of Noel storming off the US tour after having had a row with Liam. Oasis manager Marcus Russell is forced to cancel shows in San Diego, Mesa, Salt Lake City, Denver, Dallas, Austin, Kansas and

Missouri. Taking $8,000 out of the kitty, Noel flies to Las Vegas and then San Francisco to meet up with some friends. He stays in contact by phone. Some of the rest of the band and entourage stay on in the hotel in LA while others split for El Paso. They agree to reconvene in Austin, Texas.

Some of the band members are said to be suffering from the 'flu while Noel is apparently still in emotional distress after splitting up from his girlfriend of six years a couple of months ago. Noel later says: 'I thought, fuck it, we're splitting up. I got $800 (he'd claim a few months later it was actually $8,000) in cash and I got on the first plane out of LA. I had half an ounce of coke and I thought, "Right, I'm having this, then I'm going back to England. It's over.'" He adds that the LA gig was their worst ever and it was only when he saw a string of 'sold out' signs for adverts for Oasis gigs in England that he changed his mind. 'I thought that if I'd been one of the people who'd bought tickets and the band had cancelled, I'd have thought Oasis were complete c***s . . . I thought I should go back to the others and we should sort it out.'

When they get back together in Austin they record some B-sides which include *Talk tonight*. Liam describes *Talk tonight* as 'the one he [*Noel*] wrote while he was in San Francisco with some fuckin' bird, that's shit and I fuckin' hate it. That's not going on any fuckin' record of ours.' Liam says he would refuse to sing it. Initially it's meant as a B-side for *Whatever*, eventually it goes on as a B-side to *Some might say*.

The release date of *Cigarettes and alcohol* is on 10 October. It's backed by a live version of The Beatles' *I am the walrus* while the CD also features a new recording of *Fade away* and the new track *Listen up*. The cassette version is released in a cigarette-type box. The sleeve features Noel, Liam and Bonehead in a bedroom in London's Halcyon Hotel in August, hanging out with their marketing manager Tim Abbott gleefully lifting up a bottle of Becks, Creation accountant Jane Fisher sitting up in the bed, and Emma Morgan, a friend of the photographer who took the shot, Mike Jones, plucking away at a guitar. The bar bill at the £500-a-night Halcyon reputedly tops £2,000 for the evening.

Cigarettes and alcohol fails to make it as 'single of the week' in the 17 October issue of *Melody Maker*, which comes as no real surprise as rap fan Push is the reviewer. He claims it 'rips-off the Kinks and T Rex' and points out he 'can't understand the kerfuffle about such a blatantly retro sound'. *Vox* reviewer Lisa Verrico says, 'It's the most obvious teen anthem ever written. How come T Rex didn't release this years ago?'

On 14 October they play their first gig since the LA flare-up at the Uptown Bar and Grill in Minneapolis. At

one stage Liam threatens to leave the band – because Noel won't go out on the town with him! The midwest is Noel's least favourite part of America and in fact he's not too well disposed at all to our friends across the Atlantic. He once said: 'I can't see us playing at a football stadium. Unless it's in America, because I'd quite enjoy watching a load of Americans getting pneumonia or struck by lightning.'

While they are in Indianapolis for a later date

Bonehead tells Radio 1 of a close shave. 'We had a night off and Bush were playing so me and Liam were like "we'll go". We met them afterwards, it ended up in a mad one and we drank all their beer. We ended up in some club, drank some more beer. It was like four in the morning and we were staggering down this road in Indianapolis and some guy flies around the corner and just misses Liam. And Liam being Liam, he was "right, watch it dickhead". Next thing the jeep stops, this black guy, about 18 stone, pulls a gun out of his jacket pocket and goes, "What did you say?" And oh no, we're blind drunk and I was like, "Liam, chill out" and he was, "No, I'll slap him, he can't shoot me" and I was going, "I bet he can", and I was going "Come on, where's the hotel?" and we legged it around the corner and just ran.'

Noel has to go to hospital in Chicago after a 72-hour-long session when he hears *Cigarettes and alcohol* has gone in at No 7 in the UK. He is warned by the doctor to take it easy. While in the States Oasis record an unplugged-type gig for MTV's 120 minutes to be shown on 27 October and they also shoot a new video for *Supersonic* for the American market. It is filmed in various locations and is described as a mini *Man who fell to earth*. They also shoot a gig at Chicago's Metro club for a future release as a long form video (which to date still has to surface).

In the October issue of *Select* Noel reveals he is more of a realist now having experienced the euphoria of acid house only to be let down by its idealism. 'Though I never ran around bare-chested or anything like that,' he stresses to writer Andrew Perry. He also admits to an uncanny unlikelihood which will be remarked upon again and again in the future. 'They should do a puppet series and then for the one of me they could use the old one of Parker out of *Thunderbirds*.' Liam tells the same issue that 'I know for a fact, even if he [*Noel*] was going dry, he wouldn't play my songs, him.' He also points out that 'Elvis never wrote a fuckin' song in his life' and that he 'can't really write yet'.

Noel appears on a Granada TV documentary called *With Oasis* about music in Manchester. He says he has broken friends with many people since he joined the band as they now consider him 'an arrogant bastard'. 'I have lost a lot of friends,' he reflects. 'I split up with my girlfriend who I was with for six years. I have lost that and I don't think I'll ever get over it. People think we're some sort of superhuman beings who sail through life. But I get down. I've cried about some of the things that have happened to me.'

Besides Noel's rubbishing of drummer Tony McCarroll to me in Dublin, his first public hint of things to come appears in the November issue of *Vox*. When asked what his hopes and ambitions are for the next decade, among his wishes are that 'Oasis find a new drummer'. Other aspirations he'd like to see fulfilled are 'Stone Roses' second album, Man City to win something, Verve gig on the moon'. When asked what he would give Michael Jackson and Lisa Marie Presley as a wedding present he remarks, 'Albums by Blur, Suede, Shed Seven and Shampoo.'

The same issue lists *Definitely maybe* as the seventh best album of the 90s. Nirvana's *Nevermind* tops their top 50, followed by albums by Massive Attack, REM, Happy Holidays, Lemonheads and Neil Young and Crazy Horse. (Blur's *Parklife* comes in a poor 40th. One should also note that The Stone Roses' classic debut was released in 1989 and is not eligible for this particular chart.)

On 9 November Oasis turn up at the Park Lane Hotel in London for the annual *Q* awards, at which they win the Best New Act category (voted for by the magazine's readers). They lose out to Blur for Best Album and Pink Floyd for Best Live Act. Noel is pictured having a friendly chat with Damon and meets guest presenter and Labour leader Tony Blair for the first time, although he'd later reveal he was totally out of it on drugs at the time. The awards are announced in print in the January 1995 issue of *Q*.

Liam is quoted in a European magazine as saying his favourite drug is glue. 'I don't take other drugs, I prefer glue,' he insists. 'I'm not into cocaine [*although he'd later claim that when he leaves the stage he's normally 'mad for it'*]. I've got my glue, me. I don't care about the other stuff. I have been doing it since I was 14. Every day. I just keep it to myself. We don't spend hours talking about that shit.'

Noel tells the same foreign publication: 'When I was back in Manchester there was nothing else to do – playing football, taking drugs, fucking women, I suppose, and music. That's what life was like for me. If you ask me about this stuff I'll tell you the truth.' He admits drugs sometimes help him write lyrics: 'I need to be alone. I need to be in silence, have a drink and maybe some drugs. Drugs just keep me awake. They certainly helped on *Supersonic* and *Shakermaker*, which have pretty druggy lyrics.'

Noel cannot read or write music and composes his songs by singing into a walkman and strumming his guitar. He also suffers from dyslexia and admits a word over six letters can give him problems. He informs the December issue of *Select* that the reason why he and Liam are always arguing is because 'our kid tends to take everything fuckin' literally. He's a bit of a cosmic guy, a bit up in the sky. He believes in spirituality and all that. I believe in black and white.' As for Liam's singing: 'Liam's as good a singer as I am, but I can only sing acoustically. It's cool with me. He sings the way I want him to. I can't fault him. I don't think I'd let anyone else do it if it wasn't him.'

The December UK dates feature for the first time an acoustic segment with Noel playing solo on tracks such as *Sad song*. He also sports a cropped hairstyle.

Their Glasgow Barrowland date on 7 December ends in chaos with the audience booing and jeering as the set ends in confusion after just three songs. After performing *Rock 'n' roll star* and *Columbia* Liam walks offstage when he starts losing his voice during the chorus to *Fade away*. Noel announces at the end of the song that they'll attempt to get Liam back out but returns and says: 'I'm sorry, there's nothing we can do, he's lost his voice.' The band walk off and about five minutes later Noel does several songs on his own acoustically, which include *Digsy's dinner*, *Shakermaker*, *Live forever*, *Up in the sky*, *Slide away*, *Cigarettes and alcohol* and *Married with children*, with mixed reaction from the crowd. Noel again leave the stage to return with the band to play the end of the set. They play *Supersonic* and *I am the walrus*. The promoter promises anyone with ticket stub's will be let in free to a newly scheduled Barrowlands show which will take place on 27 December. Subsequent dates at Middlesbrough Town Hall and Liverpool Royal Court are called off while Liam consults a voice specialist.

The video for the Christmas single *Whatever* is shot in the first week of December at Radio 1's Maida Vale studios in London as part of a live gig for fans. The gig features an eight-piece mini-orchestra and is broadcast on the *Evening Session* on 15 December. They also appear on Channel 4's *Later With Jools Holland* on 10 December, where they perform *Whatever* and *I am the walrus* plus an acoustic version of *Sad song*.

Whatever is released on 19 December. It's delayed after David Bowie's lawyers insist Noel has nicked bits of *All the young dudes* towards the end of the track; the offending snatch is eventually erased (Oasis had already turned down a support slot to Bowie on a tour, with Noel describing him as 'an old git'). The song is embroiled in more plagiarism allegations when it's pointed out that the melody bears an uncanny resemblance to Neil Innes's 1973 hit *How sweet is an idiot*. Noel pleads innocence and says he's never even heard of the song. Creation will pay Innes ten per cent of the royalties.

Whatever is a near seven-minute Beatles-type epic complete with full string section. Noel says: 'It's the best thing I've ever written. When you hear it you just can't get it out of your head. It's possibly one of the greatest songs ever. It didn't take too long to write, about ten or 15 minutes. The song has a bit of an *All you need is love* vibe.' The number was meant to be on *Definitely maybe* and was the first 'great song' Noel admits writing. But he wanted to hang on to it until it could be recorded properly. He did not want to involve string musicians in the original recording process – cost was also a factor. He later admits it would have cost a fortune to have put it on the album due to possible royalty obligations to Innes. The single is backed by *(It's good) to be free* (which ends

with Bonehead playing an Irish jig on accordion), *Half the world away*, an acoustic number featuring Noel on vocals, and the album version of *Slide away*. Both new songs are out of the Austin sessions.

Whatever eventually sells 180,000 copies and goes to No 3 with East 17 topping the Christmas singles charts with *Stay another day*. *Whatever's* sleeve features a picture of the Derbyshire moors at Eastmoor near Sheffield. The

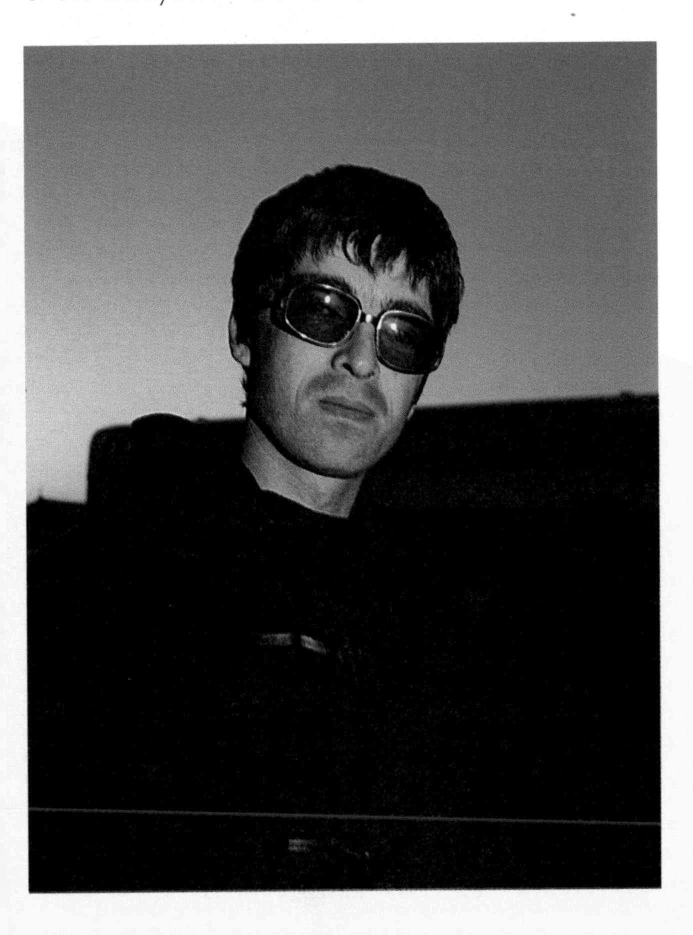

track is greeted as 'single of the week' in both *Melody Maker* and *NME* in their 17 December issues. *Melody Maker's* Everett True describes the number as 'absolutely fucking stunning ... the whole thing reeks of magnificent arrogance'. *NME's* Tommy Udo notes Oasis are far better than The Stone Roses and says the track is 'a song to die for' which 'we'll be nostalgic for in the next millennium'.

The same *NME* features Noel lining up with Pulp's Jarvis Cocker, Elastica's Justine Frischmann and Therapy?'s Andy Cairns to review some recent singles. Here are some of Noel's opinions on the following songs ... Blur's *Girls and boys*: 'A top single ... apart from *To the end* I'll buy the singles compilation when it comes out, they're a great singles band'; The Cranberries' *Zombie*: 'It's as bad as Spandau fucking Ballet's version of *Through the barricades*'; Whigfield's *Saturday night*: 'I'd love to stand in a record store and see who buys these records'; The Stone Roses' *Love spreads*: 'I like it ... nothing should take five years to record. I think it's a good tune, it's funny.' He also describes Tom Jones as 'a Welsh c***'.

NME writers rate Oasis's *Definitely maybe* as 'album of the year' in the 24/31 December issue, followed at No 2 by Blur's *Parklife*. Blur's *Girls and boys* is voted 'single of the year' while Oasis's *Cigarettes and alcohol* comes in at No 2, *Live forever* No 3, *Whatever* No 9 and *Supersonic* No 13. The edition hilariously features a 'Supersonic' boardgame in its centre pages with the likes of 'brotherly brawl' and 'your mam: go back to Burnage for a slapping'.

Melody Maker's Christmas issue chooses Portishead's *Dummy* as its 'album of the year', with Pulp No 2, Pavement No 3 and Oasis at No 4 (Blur are No 6). Blur's *Girls and boys* is also chosen as 'single of the year' with *Live forever* coming in at No 2, *Supersonic* No 12 and *Cigarettes and alcohol* No 20 (no placing for *Shakermaker*).

Everett True, reviewing the London Hammersmith gig, says *Definitely maybe* is 'unlistenable, bad metal performed by two brothers with their heads up The Roses' collective arses' but then does a u-turn to reveal, 'I love the singles though.' He adds: 'We all want to be Oasis, they're the ultimate mates, the big brothers none of us ever had – out on the town, boozin' and whorin' and livin' it up.'

The lads certainly seemed to have done plenty of that in the very rock 'n' roll year of 1994!

Getting to Number One

Oasis begin the New Year by being nominated in seven categories in the *NME* Brat awards, the magazine's alternative to the Brits. They have already won the *NME* critics' Best Album slot. Most of the other categories are voted for by *NME* readers and Oasis are up for awards for Best Album, Best New Band, Single of the Year (two nominations, for *Live forever* and *Supersonic*), Best Live Event (at London's 100 Club), Best Band and Best Radio 1 *Evening Session*.

Backstage at the awards on 23 January Liam has a little tête-à-tête with Damon Albarn. 'I'll tell ya,' says Liam, 'to your face. Your band's full of shit. Right. So I'm not going to do a photo with ya.' Damon winds Liam up by saying he doesn't want one anyway and with that Graham Coxon catches a stunned Liam by surprise by planting a kiss on his cheek. Noel announces that 'just a little thing like them [*the fans*] sticking a vote in a postbox, that means more to me than gold discs and the rest of it'. At the aftershow party in the Raw Club Noel drops one of the awards and breaks it.

Paula Yates turns up at their Brighton show and is believed to have a thing for Liam. Others who show up include Rob Newman, Menswear, Miles Hunt and Elastica. Oasis are supported by a new line-up of The La's (John Power has gone off to form Cast), who released the superb *There she goes* in the early 90s. Noel reckons The La's Lee Mavers is one of the greatest songwriters ever. At Brighton Noel introduces *Talk tonight* for the first time midway through the set.

The band announce they are pulling out of a planned Australian tour so Liam can rest his voice. Bonehead stays in Manchester as his girlfriend gives birth to their first child, Lucy Oasis. Noel is the godfather. Oasis also sell out the 12,000-capacity April show in Sheffield's Arena in just one week.

Blur outdo Oasis at the Brats. Damon and co win Best Band, Best Album, Best Single (*Girls and boys*) and Best Video (*Parklife*). Oasis have to make do with Best New Band, *NME* readers' Single of the Year (*Live forever*) and *NME* critics' Album of the Year. Oasis do, however pick up the critics' 'album of the year' in the January editions of both *Select* and *Vox* with Blur coming in second. They also win Vox's 'Single of the Year' for *Supersonic*.

Oasis head back to America and Noel cuts his head open during a freak go-karting accident at Virginia Beach, Virginia. He is rushed to hospital for stitches to his head, having collided into another go-kart in a seven-car race. The incident takes place during a break in their 25-gig tour of America. *Melody Maker* reviewer Sarah Le Claire is at their gig in Virginia Beach and notes, 'They walk the walk of men who are clearly on the threshold of greatness, accompanied solely on their own terms, and they know it . . . city by city, the United States is theirs for the taking.'

The band appear on the coast-to-coast David Letterman show and perform *Live forever*. They reach No 58 in the US album charts with *Definitely maybe*, shifting 400,000 copies. Noel declares that Oasis are 'the best equipped band from England to come to the USA' but stresses that 'America is no more important than anywhere else in the world'. Little known UK outfit Nirvana, who got some cash off Kurt Cobain's band a few years ago for unknowingly using the same name, threaten a law suit against Oasis as they claim *Whatever* bears an uncanny resemblance to a song of theirs, *Tiny goddess*.

The February edition of *Select* results in a close race between Oasis and Blur for the honours in the annual readership poll. Blur win band of the year and album of the year with Oasis coming second. But Oasis win best live act and have the two top singles, *Live forever* and *Supersonic*, while *Cigarettes and alcohol* is at No 5. Oh, Liam also wins the 'twat of the year' award, narrowly beating off British Defence Minister Michael Portillo and

Marshall
Marshall
Marshall

Liam's good mate Evan Dando (Damon is a surprising 11th while Noel is 6th).

Phil Redmond, the creator of Brookside – Noel and girlfriend Meg Matthews are big fans – tells the 11 February issue of *Melody Maker* that Oasis's version of *I am the walrus* is one of his favourite songs. 'It's a great version, and I like it because I can listen to it without all the scouse angst and scouseology I have to go through when I actually play The Beatles,' he says cryptically. 'My Beatles records are in pristine condition because I never play them – you don't need to! In Liverpool you hear The Beatles in every pub and shop you go into.'

First word comes through that Oasis will headline one of the nights at Glastonbury with Soundgarden and Smashing Pumpkins on the other two nights. Then on 22 February the band starts a three-day stint at Loco studios in south Wales (why is it that all the top studios seem to be in Wales?!). They're there to record a new single *Some might say*, out on 24 April. It was written last June, around the same time as *Whatever*. Noel jokes that the new single rips off The Faces' *Ooh la la*. They also record two B-sides, *Acquiesce* and *Headshrinker* which together with *Talk tonight* will be additional tracks with the single. Owen Morris produces. Noel and Liam sing alternative verses on *Acquiesce* (Noel can be heard singing 'What's the story morning glory?' at its beginning) while the acoustic *Talk tonight* (Liam's favourite track – not!) is sung by Noel. Noel discloses he heard the word 'acquiesce' for the first time while watching the O.J. Simpson trial and wrote the song in 20 minutes while on a broken-down train in the Severn tunnel on the way to the studio.

During a break in recording Liam involves himself in a flare-up at Manchester's trendy Dry 201 Bar. After four hours of drinking double gins and tonic he allegedly starts abusing a female customer. The woman's male companion takes exception and hits Liam, kicking off a fracas. Liam and his friend are also accused of throwing glasses and ashtrays around the bar while Liam is further said to have vomited on a table. The duo are finally ejected from the bar before they have another confrontation outside with a taxi driver. The Dry Bar incident is caught on closed circuit monitors and later broadcast by *The Word*.

The bar manager, Leroy Richardson, tells *Manchester Evening News*: 'Liam and a mate had been in from three o'clock in the afternoon. It seems the trouble started when Liam was rude to another customer's girlfriend. The man and Liam had words, and Liam's general attitude seemed to be that he was a pop star and could do what he liked. Liam and his friend were worse for wear, and started throwing glasses and ashtrays and broke a £70 vase. His mate even tried to throw a table. Liam told me, "I'm 'ard. I'm tough". I had no choice but to throw them out.' The bar was the same one where Shaun Ryder smashed a mirror in 1990 and he too was ejected by Richardson, who said then: 'The clientele are well-behaved. It's just the pop stars we have to watch out for.'

Oasis are rumoured, and a couple of weeks later confirmed, to be playing the main stage at Glastonbury on Friday 23 June. Blur win a record-breaking four awards at the Brits on 28 February (band, single, video, album). Oasis win the best newcomer slot and dedicate their award to George Martin, the legendary Beatles producer. He later approaches the band and proposes a collaboration.

Noel and the whole Oasis table (bar Liam, who was reputedly in the toilet shouting at his reflection!) jump and start grooving to Blur's live performance of *Girls and boys*. Damon announces from the stage that Blur should be jointly accepting the best band award that really they should be accepting it with Oasis and adds kids should go up to their teachers with Blur and Oasis albums proclaiming, 'This is my education.' Noel later decrees: 'If we had won that, none of our lot would have said what he did. Our lot would have said "fuck the lota ya". What Blur did was a great gesture and I want to go on record saying that it's us and them now, us and them against the world.'

They head back to the States where *Live forever* has topped the college radio charts and *Definitely maybe* has sold over 200,000 copies. At their New York gig on 3 March tennis player John McEnroe shows up backstage. Liam describes him as 'completely off his tits, fucking mad'. The Gallaghers' brother Paul and mother Peggy fly over for the show.

Oasis appear on Channel 4's *The White Room* on 13 April and play *Some might say*, *Good to be free* and *Acquiesce*. Noel, on acoustic guitar, also does a duet with Paul Weller, on piano. They play *Talk tonight*. PJ Harvey is on the same show, as Bobby Womack and CJ Lewis. Also hanging around are Chris Evans, Kylie Minogue (who only stays to watch PJ and then leaves), Mark Lamarr plus Paula Yates and Michael Hutchence (it's the first public spotting of the pair together since she questioned him on her bed on *The Big Breakfast* and inevitably leads to a full-blown affair and divorce from Bob Geldof). Eyewitnesses claim that after momentarily ditching Hutchence, Paula manages to barge her way into the Oasis dressing-room and allegedly tries it on with Liam asking him, 'What do you think of me now that I'm single?'. Liam reportedly persuades her to get back with the INXS star. 'I can't believe it,' Liam says as he angrily bolts the door behind her, 'she's old enough to be my mother.' Paula later angrily denies chatting Liam up.

The bust-up that everyone predicted between Oasis and Tony McCarroll finally happens in Paris on 19 April. Liam and Tony have an altercation in a bar which leads to a bloody punch-up. They are thrown out with their entourage.

The release of *Some might say* is on 24 April. The sleeve depicts Cromford railway station, a small stop on the Matlock to Derby line. The station may appear disused to casual observers but it's been cropped to hide the fact that trains do actually turn up.

The Tony saga does not rest and on 1 May Oasis's management announce that the band has parted company with Tony McCarroll. Ignition say he wasn't sacked and that the parting was by mutual consent. Just two weeks previously a band spokesman denied rumours of an impending split, stressing that 'Oasis exists as a unit and Tony is crucial to the band'. They repeat a couple of times over the following week that the split has nothing to do with the punch-up and stress again it's by 'mutual consent'. Noel will later say he felt Tony's drumming was not up to scratch and he would not be able to play the new songs.

The night before Oasis had just stormed into the singles charts with their first No 1, *Some might say*. They've knocked fellow Mancunians Take That's *Back for good* off the top spot. A jubilant Noel says: 'It proves that we've done everything we said we would, and it's as much a success for our fans as it is for us. There are ten bands in the top ten, five in the top five, but there's only one at No 1.' After attending a Heavenly Records bash at the Flamingo bar in London he and Guigsy return to Noel's flat to ring up Liam and Bonehead in Manchester to celebrate over the phone. By the way, the previous week Oasis and The Verve had spent an evening in a Paris bar around the

Oasis's engine room: Guigsy and Bonehead.

time of the Liam and Tony punch-up singing Take That songs all night, or so we're told!

But more seriously, Oasis are due on *Top of the Pops* later this week and have no drummer. Noel tells Radio 1: 'Everyone was going, "What have we done?" We were also due to start the album that Friday. That Tuesday afternoon I met Alan.' The 'Alan' is Alan White (born 26 May 1972), younger brother of Steve White, longstanding drummer with Paul Weller's band. Alan himself has been a proficient drummer for some years and the young south Londoner comes highly recommended, having played previously with Creation signing Idha.

'I went back to see my Mum and says, "Any calls?"' he remembers. 'She said, "Oh, Noel someone from Oasis, is it?"' Alan immediately goes around for an audition. 'I probably wasn't as nervous as I should have been because I didn't have time to think,' he explains.

Noel recalls: 'So it suddenly dawned on me about five minutes before he was due to turn up, what if he weighs about 32 stone? Anyway, he came around the corner and as soon as he shook my hand I said, "You're in." and he went, "Oh, don't you want to know what my musical influences are?" and I went, "No, mate, you're under 13 stone, you'll do for me, you're in." He said, "Right, when do I start?", and I said, "You start tomorrow morning, you're on *Top of the Pops*." I gave him the CD [*Some might say*] and said, "You better have that worked out by tomorrow morning" and he went, "Cheers, mate" and that was that.'

Liam appears on the cover of the 22 April issue of *Melody Maker* with the blurb: 'Oasis: their first major interview of 1995'. Noel tells Paul Mathur: 'I hate people who say they only write songs for themselves and if anyone else likes them it's a bonus. If people don't love Oasis, they're shit.' He also reveals that he recently recorded with Paul Weller for the first time, playing a cover of Dr John's *Walk on gilded splinters*. They record it at The Manor in Oxfordshire for Weller's new album *Stanley Road*.

The same issue of *Melody Maker* has Everett True reviewing *Some might say* which, he says, 'begins – and continues – like every other Oasis single you've heard (or The Faces/Primal Scream/T Rex – delete as applicable)' but concedes it's 'so obviously single of the week it's not even worth putting a picture next to the review'. (Two weeks later, the same magazine's David Stubb posthumously awards the track 'single of the week' – 'It's No 1 and we should throw a party of our own to match the VE day bash . . . *Some might say* is Oasis's best yet.'

They play a warm-up show at Southend cliffs pavilion just before the mega Sheffield date. The Southend show features almost everything the fans know, except *Whatever*. Liam dedicates *Slide away* to the ladies and gushes 'I love girls'. The show is recorded and later released as an 80-minute-long form video called *Oasis: Live by the sea*.

In the follow-up Oasis piece with Paul Mathur in *Melody Maker* Liam tells the 29 April issue that he's not that bitter against Blur. 'I don't like what they're doing musically but they're alright. They're mad for it and I like them for that.' Noel hints there may be an Oasis B-sides album in the offing 'later this year', which he again repeats in 1996. Noel says his battles with Liam are hyped but contends his younger brother thinks 'he's at war with the world, but I'm not sure why, there's something really getting to him, but I don't know what it is. He's always questioning everything . . . he wants to know the answers right now.'

Liam reveals: 'I live for now, not for what happens after I die. If I die and there's something afterwards, I'm going to hell, not to heaven. I mean, the devil's got all the good gear. What's God got? The Inspiral Carpets and nuns. Fuck that. On my grave I want them to write, "Don't come here with your bunches of flowers." I don't want a gravestone, I want a V-sign, two fingers . . . when you're dead, you're dead. It's now that matters.' He also complains that Noel thinks the band are like sheep – 'if he told them all to turn up tomorrow because he'd got a plan that we were going to play a gig up a lamp-post, they'd all just do it' – and adds it hurt when Noel once told him that if Liam wrote a song like *Hey Jude* he'd quit.

The 6 May issue carries a review of Oasis's Sheffield Arena gig by David Bennun. 'They must feel like The Beatles at Shea stadium, which surely is what the

Gallagher brothers want most of all out of life,' he writes. 'Tonight is a triumph.' They also unveil *Don't look back in anger* for the first time.

Noel appears as one of 100 stars in the June issue of *Q* in a feature on 'the record that changed my life'. He chooses The Sex Pistols' *Never mind the bollocks*. 'It came out when I was 11 but I didn't actually hear it until I was about 13. I'd been playing guitar for a while, so when that came out I had to learn all the guitar riffs because all the guitar parts were easy to play – *Pretty vacant, Bodies, EMI, God save the queen*, all of them were my favourites really. If you think that all punk music was supposed to be the anti-music, *Never mind the bollocks* sounds like a pop album in comparison. My mum fucking hated it. Very Catholic, so she didn't approve of tracks like *Bodies*. It had to be really good if she didn't like it. She even used to hide the record from me, so I had to buy it on tape and hide it in my pocket.'

On 8 May they book into Rockfield studios in Wales to begin recording the album and stay ensconced there until 17 June. Six tracks for the album, provisionally titled *Morning glory*, are. laid with Owen Morris. The tracks include: *Champagne supernova, All around the world, The red, white and blue* and *Don't look back in anger*. As we know by now two of those tracks did not make the finished product. *All around the world* is the 11-minute epic Noel threatens to unleash on the Eurovision Song Contest. Even more curiously, Liam revealed earlier in the year that *The red, white and blue* is being saved for the third album and Noel admitted it may be 'controversial' as he hinted that it's anti-protest marchers and anti-vegetarianism and the like. Hopefully, it doesn't turn out to be a jingoistic, nationalistic affront aka his Union Jack guitar, more of which later.

During these sessions Noel takes off to Jersey for a week, having had another row with Liam. His kid brother one night brings back 'half of South Wales with him' and Noel moans that he doesn't want the studio turned into '*National Lampoon's Animal House*'. 'Me and Owen would work 15 hours a day, but because the rest of them would put on their stuff last they'd just go around the pub,' Noel tells Radio 1. 'But one night they brought half of South Wales back with them and there was all these kids running around the studio and all that and somebody smashed a window in the studio and it got a bit out of order.'

Liam claims he had a right to bring people back: 'He had a row with me about his ignorance towards people he didn't know and I told him to shut up and walk home . . . I said I don't talk to people like that who I know you don't know because I'll slap you around miles. So we had a fight and that was it. Then I trashed the place, yeah, because I went right off my tits.'

Poor Owen Morris is again caught in the middle. 'They've split up twice on sessions that I've recorded and it's all about nothing,' he explains. 'They always end up getting back together and next day it's like nothing's happened, which is really weird. They love each other, really. I'm absolutely convinced that Liam loves Noel more than anybody else, possibly even himself. As to who Noel loves, I don't know.'

While in Jersey Noel stays at Blackburn footballer Graham Le Saux's house and has his picture taken with Graham's championship medal, which he intends posting back to his Man Utd mates. Noel had struck up a friendship with Le Saux during his time with Inspiral Carpets. 'The best thing about football is that United lost the championship because I fucking hate them,' he says. 'We were here [*in Wales*] watching them lose it and it was a monumental occasion.'

A girl comes up to Noel in Jersey to ask for an autograph and says she'll see him in Glastonbury. Noel is bemused that she'll travel so far to a festival but she explains her dad is playing there – Gilbert O'Sullivan! 'I was like, "That old c***",' he sniggers. 'And her mum grabbed my arm and said, "Easy, that's my husband."'

Oasis's *Live forever* is included on a Glastonbury 25th anniversary album. Other acts on it include Blur, New Order, Primal Scream, Sinead O'Connor, Paul Weller and Billy Bragg. An Oasis official live CD appears in British shops, called simply *Oasis live*. It was recorded at Chicago's Metro theatre on 12 October 1994. It is packaged to look like a bootleg and is released by Epic America (Oasis's US record company). The album features 13 tracks – the whole of *Definitely maybe*, plus *Fade away* and an extended nine-minute version of *I am the walrus*. Liam and Noel can also be heard arguing, as ever, over the order of the set list.

Noel announces in the 17 June *NME* that Oasis may only record a maximum of three albums. 'I don't see us going on for ever,' he says. 'I see it as three albums and that's it. I don't think I can do any more with Oasis after that. There's only so many anthems you can write. I don't know for sure, but I'd say the next album [*the third*] will be the last.'

Early in June Oasis reach an 'amicable settlement' with the clothing firm of the same name. Noel and Liam can be seen pictured outside one of the branches in a famous shot by Manchester photographer Kevin Cummins. The once-only payment is never officially revealed but is believed to be a low six-figure price. Noel once claimed that the band was actually named after a branch in Manchester, which Liam naturally disputes.

They play a secret Glastonbury warm-up gig at Bath's Pavilion on 22 June where they premiere *Roll with it*. They shoot the sleeve for the new single on a beach at Weston super Mare the next morning. On 23 June they headline the Friday night slot of Glastonbury. Noel has a cold and wears a duffel coat onstage while Liam is in foul humour and asks the crowd for a fight. The gig is a bitter let-down and disappointment. 'This is the most ragged kind of Glasters glory,' writes Simon Williams in *NME*. 'Occasionally unpleasant, frequently arrogant, sometimes inspirational and quite probably racing off its nuts, the Oasis machine rumbles to a halt with *Live forever*.'

Noel would say later: 'I think we froze at Glastonbury. I did, personally. Halfway through the gig I thought we didn't really want to be there. I thought it was unfair that we were put under that pressure to pull the whole festival off and when it didn't happen people were slagging us off for it.'

The backstage malarkey was all the more remarkable because of the antics of Oasis's new-found mate, Robbie Williams of Take That. The clearly out of it peroxide blond-haired star was pictured getting sick lying sozzled on the ground. He was invited onstage that night for his little 15 minutes of fame. But his management and the rest of Take That were horrified at the damage to their squeaky clean image and on 17 July, having seen relations break down between him and the others for various reasons, he is promptly sacked.

While he was onstage at Glastonbury Noel wore a duffel coat and the band also wear them for the cover of *Roll with it*. It's later reported that clothing firm Gloverall has experienced a 20 per cent surge in sales of the garments.

Noel jokes in the 24 June *NME* that Paul Weller is 'a moany old bastard. He's like Victor Meldrew with a suntan. He's a nice bloke. I love him like the day is long and he's honest. Too honest maybe.' He complains that Pulp's *Common people* should have gone to No 1. 'The lyrics are hilarious, I think he [*Jarvis*] is a top guy,' he points out. He also reveals he's listening to Black Grape, Dodgy and '*Stanley Road*, obviously'. He bumped into Tricky at a Massive Attack gig and the Bristol musician suggested a collaboration. 'Tricky was saying we should be doing some stuff together,' Noel elaborates. 'I said, "Sure, if you've got the razor blade and the mirror." But he meant music, unfortunately!'

He also discloses that he bumped into Morrissey on a street in Camden and was a little afraid of him as he got closer due to unkind words he had said in the past about Mozzer. One of Noel's favourite early gigs was when he first saw The Smiths at the Free Trade Hall in Manchester in 1984 and was amazed at all the flowers

there and also the girls. Anyway, the two stop and chat and Moz asks if Noel is having a party given that he's got a bag of booze with him. Noel feels incumbent to invite him along to his birthday party but is secretly dreading the thought of the man with the quiff turning up. 'Next thing this card appears through the letterbox from Morrissey saying, "Sorry, I can't make it, but give us a ring if you want to go shoplifting" . . . Sarcastic little c***, but I can dig that.'

Noel complains to the July issue of *Vox* that he is not nominated for an Ivor Novello award despite 'having five fuckin' top ten hits and now a No 1'. The Ivor Novello award is given to the best songwriter of the year and Noel rates it more highly than the Brits. 'That was the award I wanted more than the fuckin' others,' he moans. 'But you know, I just won't turn up next year when they gift it to me. They can fuck right off. They'll have to give it to me Mam instead. Actually, no, I take that back, I will be there.' A year later Noel does indeed win the Ivor Novello award – but with Blur. He announces he will not show up for the awards and appeals to Blur to do likewise as he insists the organisers have deliberately worked out the dual award as a cheap publicity stunt. He also says elsewhere in the same issue: 'People go on about us and Blur but they're out-and-out pop music. We're out-and-out rock music . . . but Suede are shit and I fuckin' hate them. And Elastica. And Echobelly. And Menswear. I want to stop slagging other bands off 'cos I've met most of them now and they're really nice people. But I have to be honest and say they're not very good.'

Noel reveals to Tom Doyle in the July issue of *Q* that he once got strip-searched at Manchester airport with Mark Coyle when some members of their group got nicked for having cannabis on them after touching down on a separate flight from Amsterdam. 'So they went through the list of all the people in the party and found out there was two left,' he explains. 'Next day we're waltzing through the airport, stoned as a pair of c***s, and they said, "Can you come over here please?" We didn't have anything, but they strip-searched us and all that shit, which was pretty horrible. Not quite finger-up-the-arse, just a quick look.' He also confesses: 'Our Liam and Damon don't get on at all, they tend to wind each other up. But I like Damon, he's alright.'

The band heads north to Scotland to play two sell-out shows in a big top at a beach near Irvine. On 22 July they arrive in Ireland, having flown in from Belgium. They take a helicopter, their first time in one, to Slane Castle, Co. Meath, 30 miles to the west of Dublin. It's a natural amphitheatre on the banks of the River Boyne, overlooked by a medieval castle. Johnny Depp and Helena Christensen turn up. They hear the album has finally been satisfactorily cut at Abbey Road studios in London on 25 July.

The Battle of Britpop: Blur versus Oasis

Oasis had planned to release their new single *Roll with it* on 14 August while Blur were rumoured to be scheduling to release their new track *Country house* on 21 August. Both bands would have expected to go straight in at No 1 with the respective numbers one week after the other. But soon the Oasis camp are aghast when they learn that Blur's record company, Food, has decided the release date of *Country house* will also be 14 August, setting up a straight head-to-head battle between the two crown princes of Britpop. (The phrase 'Britpop' had been used by critics to tag the type of guitar-orientated music which had developed after the 'Madchester' dance boom and baggy era.) Even in the days of The Beatles and The Rolling Stones in the 60s both bands' record companies used to agree release dates which would avoid clashes between each other's respective singles.

Blur had initially planned to release *Stereotypes* as their first single from their forthcoming album *The great escape* but settled on *Country house* after positive feedback from their recent Mile End stadium gig. Their producer, Stephen Street, also felt it would be a better summer record. Neither Blur nor their record company expected any releases from Oasis during August. As *Morning glory* will not be out for several weeks Damon is astounded when he hears Oasis's scheduling for the new single and is sure they're doing it deliberately to upset Blur's plans. After a series of phone calls between both record companies, both bands bullishly decide on a head-to-head with neither ready to give way.

Blur have never had a No 1 single while Noel wants to equal or better his hero Paul Weller's four No 1s with The Jam. Although Oasis have a bigger base, with an official fan club membership of an estimated 130,000 people, Blur are on a high, having played the Mile End show and supported REM at Milton Keynes, while music insiders and DJs indicate that *Country house* would appeal to a far bigger mainstream audience than *Roll with it*. Blur also, cunningly, release two CD versions of their single with different B-sides on each release so that many of their fans would be inclined to buy both. Noel is adamant about the outcome and says Blur 'are middle-class wankers trying to lay hard ball with a bunch of working-class heroes'.

When Chris Evans played Oasis's *Roll with it* to Damon Albarn over the air down a telephone one morning the Blur singer could be heard chuckling in the background and singing 'And I like it, I like it, I like it, I l-iii-iiike it . . . li-iiiiike it, here we go', to the air of Status Quo's *Rockin' all over the world*. Even more provocatively, one of the lines to *Country house* reads: 'Now he's got morning glory/life's a different story'. Damon told me recently it was pure coincidence and he just wanted something to rhyme with 'story'.

Oasis take a break and pop over to Ireland to support REM at Slane Castle outside Dublin. While there Noel informs George Byrne of the *Irish Independent* that under no circumstances would he pen a tune with Blur for England for the European football championships. 'Over my dead body,' he says. 'We're Irish. Let Blur do it, they're English.' When pressed on the roots question several months later by Mike Edgar of BBC Radio Ulster, and specifically that quote, Noel makes a mini U-turn and declares, 'We're British, we're English.'

Towards the end of July Blur are playing the Feile festival in Cork and I approach Damon. Having heard *Country house* but not *Roll with it*, I ask him what the Oasis track is like as he lazes in the sun. He smiles and his mate says, 'Have you heard of Status Quo?' Damon smirks and splutters, 'I didn't say that.' I asked him about a possible link-up between Oasis and Blur for the England theme tune for Euro '96. 'Oasis shouldn't do it. They're Irish,' he smiled. 'Oasis should do the Irish one. It would go down better in America.' As we know by now Ireland failed to make it to the finals.

Liam hits back by branding Blur and *Country house* as 'Chas and Dave chimney-sweep music' . . . Damon: 'Oasis quo' . . . Liam: 'A bunch of middle-class art students.'

NME gear up for the battle royal by tagging the clash on the front of their 12 August edition (complete with old-style boxers in a masthead): 'British heavyweight championship – Blur vs Oasis, August 14, the big chart showdown.' But reviewer Mark Sutherland in the same edition gives some indication of the lie of the land by proclaiming Blur 'single of the week' and Oasis 'not single of the week'. 'The last two singles in Oasis's ludicrously intensive campaign suggest prolific workrate is finally taking a toll on Noel Gallagher's once seemingly bottomless well of cracking choons,' Sutherland warns. He draws similarities to a couple of Status Quo tracks and although conceding it's a 'pretty good' track, he stresses '"pretty good" isn't quite good enough to be the Best Band in Britain'. Blur's *Country house*, on the other hand, he proclaims is 'a knockout'.

Damon points out in the 19 August *Melody Maker*: 'More than competition with Oasis, it's competition with ourselves. We've never had a Number One single. We want one.' Both bands plaster the music papers with full-page adverts for their singles.

As the big countdown ticks away the battle in the pop charts remarkably makes it into the mainstream media. Nothing like this has happened with pop in over a generation as the clash catches a nation's imagination. *Roll with it* is accompanied by the B-sides *It's better people*, *Rockin' chair* and a live recording from Glastonbury of *Live forever*.

Oasis had been confident their hardcore fan base would win the day but soon the jitters begin with news that there are problems with the printing of bar codes on copies of *Roll with it*. To register as many copies as possible electronically, and thus increase sales and chart position, these bar codes are essential for reading by the Gallup-monitored machines in selected stores. The problem is only spotted during routine checks and four days before release 80 staff work through the night at the distribution factory to stick new bar codes on 100,000 copies of the single. But one major store contacted in

Noel meets a few of his fans (Slane 1995).

London midweek during the clash admits there are still problems and many Oasis sales are not registering. Oasis are reported to be 'furious'. Oasis's campaign is not helped by the fact that *Roll with it* is £1 dearer than *Country house*.

The likes of the *Sun*, the *Daily Mirror* and the *Daily Star* even run tallies during the days after the singles go on sale on 14 August. The general opinion appears to be that Blur are in the lead. 'Blur grab lead in big pop battle,' heralds Linda Duff in the *Daily Star*. Even the *Financial Times*, *The Times*, the *Independent*, *The Guardian*, the *Daily Mail* and the *Daily Express* all feel incumbent to cover the story, dedicating large features and even front-page write-offs and blurbs. Pointedly, *The Times* even feels it necessary to write an editorial on the Britpop war in its 15 August edition, proclaiming, 'Weep not Lycidas – for today's the day Britain's musical youth is having its picnic . . . whoever wins, pop's greatest purpose will be served – the making of large amounts of money.'

The *Sun* announces that there will be another battle forthcoming in Bournemouth on 18 September as both bands will be playing the seaside resort. In a mods versus rockers flashback to the 60s it hints there could be trouble between both bands' fans if they played the venues, within several hundred yards of each other, on the same night. Oasis will later pull out of the gig in the much larger venue citing safety reasons.

The media scramble gets so bizarre that by Saturday the *Sun* is reporting in a three-page story, splashed 'You Blur-ty rat', that Bristol Oasis fan Mandy Vivian-Thomas had kicked her husband, Richard, a Blur fan, out of their marital home after he had microwaved her CDs!

Blur also outdo Oasis in terms of TV exposure. Significantly, BBC's six o'clock news covers the story with a backdrop behind newsreader John Humphreys depicting the Blur and Oasis logos before a film piece which includes interviews with both Damon and Liam and members of the public. On the Wednesday Damon presented *Britpop* on BBC2, featuring Blur performing *Country house* and a who's who of Britpop, including Sleeper, Pulp and Supergrass. Oasis are rather pettily omitted.

Oasis perform *Roll with it* on *Top of the Pops* with Noel singing and Liam playing guitar (it is mimed after all and they like taking the piss). Blur's £50,000 video for *Country house* plays out the closing credits. It's also wall-to-wall TV coverage from ITV's *The Chart Show* to Channel 4's *The Big Breakfast*.

On Sunday afternoon, 21 August, both bands are informed of their placings. The rest of us have to tune in to Radio 1 to hear the countdown with just several minutes to go to 7 p.m. As the top 40 is listed off DJ Mark Goodier sneakily announces: '. . . so it's moment of truth time, the UK's No 2 song is Blur . . . or Oasis, which do you think? OK, I'll tell you, it's Oasis at No 2 . . .' Oasis fans had been in high heaven for a millisecond with the initial intimation that 'the UK's No 2 song is Blur . . .' only to be deflated immediately, even feeling cheated. It's only the third time in pop history that the top two slots have been filled by new entries.

Damon had been told the result earlier in the afternoon just before he had gone to play football. Asked about the problem with Oasis's bar codes, he replies: 'Well, it was Oasis that wanted to play it this way. They started all this. At the end of the day they had just as many records in the shops, but we sold more.' It finally emerges that *Country house* sold 270,000 copies that week, *Roll with it* 220,000. Nearly 500,000 of the 1.8 million singles sold that week had been made up by Blur and Oasis.

Oasis were in Japan during the announcement. Noel, naturally dismayed, would later say he'd never forgive Damon for the head-to-head contest, claiming Blur brought their release date forward deliberately to collide with Oasis. Liam appears to have made up somewhat with Damon. Even though Oasis now outsell Blur by almost three to one in the album charts, Noel still bitterly dislikes Blur, showing only a modicum of fondness for Graham Coxon. Noel will later remark to San Francisco's *Bay Area Magazine*: 'The thing that gets me is, people will say they're [*Blur*] The Beatles and we're The Stones. The fact of the matter is we're The Beatles AND The Stones and they're the fuckin' Monkees, man.' He will later stress: 'I will never resolve my differences with that bloke [*Damon*] . . . I don't think there's anything that c*** could say that would redeem him in my eyes. That lot from Blur are fucking two- faced.' But he does admit he feels sorry for fans of both bands as, if he was 16, he'd probably like both. On the other hand Damon says: 'They'll [*Oasis*] look back on it when they're grown men and just think what dickheads they were.'

At a charity football match at the Mile End stadium in London in May 1996 both Oasis and Blur enter teams. While Patsy Kensit watches from the sidelines both sides are knocked out. But as a crowd pleaser Liam and Damon walk hand in hand back on to the pitch and the teams play each other. Liam jokingly tries to pull down Damon's shorts. Blur win 2–0. Noel does not show up.

What's the Story Oasis?

Oasis put the disappointment of losing the battle against Blur behind them and Noel immediately throws himself into the Bosnian children's charity project 'War Child', a subject close to his heart. But at first he expresses reservations about the way the project is being handled by Robbie Williams on Channel 4's *The Big Breakfast* in a phone interview from Japan, although he soon becomes immersed in the venture.

A string of top bands agree to come together to record a track each for free on 5 September for an album to be rush released on 9 September. Former Stone Roses guitarist John Squire did the coverwork for the album free too (he also did the cover for *The second coming*). Many bands are out of Britain during the recording but the likes of Blur have booked recording time in Milan that day, Radiohead are in a studio in America while Therapy?, PJ Harvey and Terrorvision also record abroad. Former Nirvana bassist Krist Novoselic writes the sleeve notes for the record and Brian Eno, a 'War Child' patron, is executive producer. A total of 19 acts participate on 20 tracks and the album is titled *Help*. The project is the brainchild of Go! Discs' Tony Crean who read a newspaper one day which spelled out the appalling condition of thousands of children in war-ravaged Bosnia.

At one minute past midnight on 5 September Noel is the first artist to begin recording for the album. He's helped by Johnny Depp on guitar, Lisa Moorish, whom Liam is later romantically linked with, on backing vocals, while Alan White is on drums. They record a new version of *Fade away* at Abbey Road studios, where The Beatles recorded many of their finest works. Later in the day Noel teams up with Paul Weller to record a version of The Beatles' *Come together*. Paul McCartney unexpectedly turns up to contribute backing vocals to the track, 33 years to the day since he first went to the studio to record *Love me do* with the famous Liverpool group. The trio call themselves The Mojo Filters with Noel playing rhythm guitar. 'I think the whole idea is fucking great,' he says. Noel later remarks on his encounter with a real life Beatle: 'We talked about how weird it is to be in a band that never never gets to see your own band perform live. He said, "Does it piss you off?" and I said, "Well, you were in The Beatles, man!" Imagine being in The Beatles and never seeing *The Beatles*.'

When the album's released on 9 September it sells 71,000 copies in just one day, more than any album sells that whole week and generates £1 million from advance orders for the charity. But it is not eligible for the UK album charts as it is a compilation, causing ripples of complaints from those involved.

Oasis also announce the biggest ever indoor concert not only in Britain, but in Europe too. Earls Court will be the venue for a 20,000-capacity gig on 5 November. Demand is later so intense a second show is added and it too sells out within hours.

Oasis are soon rocked by the news that Paul McGuigan has nervous exhaustion and cannot play, having fallen ill. On 11 September they postpone their upcoming UK tour. 'The poor guy just needs a bit of a lie down,' says Noel. The band reschedules their UK tour dates (including Bournemouth which is pushed forward to 5 October). Noel explains they had just finished recording the album, now called *(What's the story) morning glory?*, and went straight to Japan. When they returned Paul did not show up for rehearsals. He insists the illness had nothing to do with drugs and points out Guigsy only smokes a bit of pot and that his doctor was more concerned about his diet. They decide to give him the rest of the year off and audition for a replacement bass player.

They fail to win the Mercury Music prize of £25,000 for album of the year. It goes instead to Portishead's *Dummy*, although the band did turn up for the reception on 12 September. It's at these awards that Liam verbally assaults Justine Frischmann of Elastica, Damon Albarn's

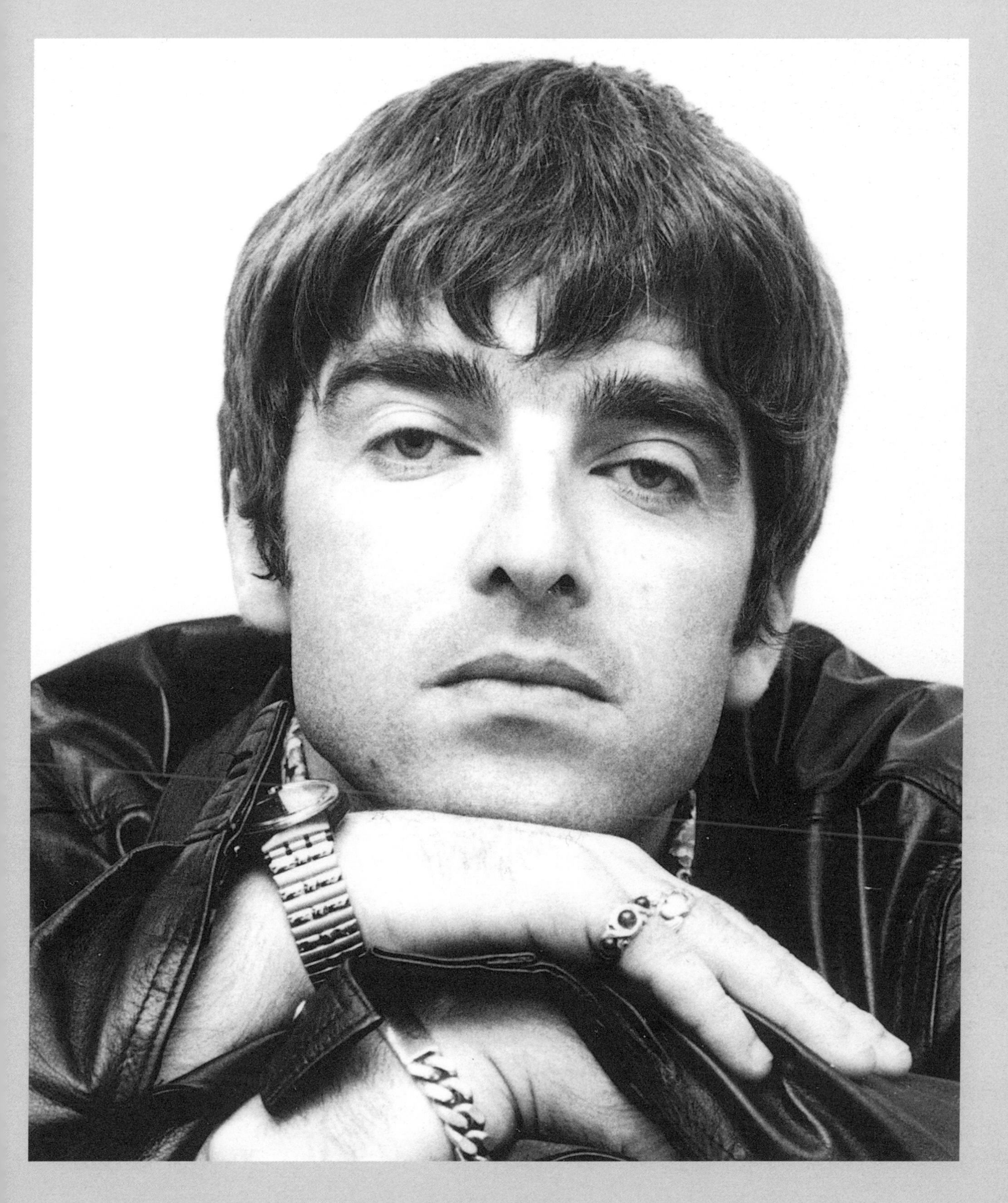

Liam hears there is a strike by coke dealers (joke!).

girlfriend. He tells her to 'get your tits out' and insinuates that she'd really like to go to bed with him.

Oasis's planned show on 18 September at the Bournemouth International Centre is changed to the following evening due to pressure from the police. They had sold 4,300 tickets for the gig while Blur were also due to play the same town that night at a much smaller 700-capacity venue. Oasis's management claim they approached Blur to move their show along with Oasis to a different night as a compromise on safety grounds. They claim Blur would not co-operate so they act unilaterally.

On 17 September a slightly drunk and worse for wear Noel puts his foot in it big time when an interview with him appears in the *Observer's* supplement magazine. Naturally still enraged after the Blur versus Oasis show-down and defeat he conducts a no-holds-barred interview on the phone from Japan with journalist Miranda Sawyer. Asked about Blur, he says: 'The guitarist [*Graham Coxon]* I've got a lot of time for. The drummer [*Dave Rowntree*] I've never met – I hear he's a nice guy. The bass player [*Alex James*] and the singer – I hope the pair of them catch AIDS and die because I fucking hate them two.' The interview also contains further over-the-top remarks about Blur which border on libel while Noel claims, 'I'm on a line of coke every 40 minutes now' (which he later denies). His remarks draw a furious reaction from charities involved with people who are HIV positive or have AIDS, with the Terence Higgins Trust to the forefront of condemnation. Blur's record company bosses also lash out at Noel over the outburst and Food supremo Andy Ross even goes so far as to describe Noel as 'the fuckwit from up north'.

Two weeks later a genuinely remorseful Noel makes a fulsome apology for the AIDS-related remarks. He issues the following statement: 'I would like to apologise to all concerned at my comments about Damon Albarn and Alex James in an *Observer* article printed last Sunday. The off-the-cuff remark was made last month at the height of a "war of words" between both bands, and it must have been the 50th time during the interview that I was pressed to give an opinion of Blur. As soon as I said it, I realised it was an insensitive thing to say as AIDS is no joking matter, and immediately retracted the comment, but was horrified to pick up the *Observer* and find the journalist concerned chose to still run with it. Anyone who knows me will confirm that I've always been sympathetic towards the plight of HIV carriers and AIDS sufferers, as well as being supportive of the challenge to raise awareness about AIDS and HIV. Although not being a fan of their music, I wish both Damon and Alex a long and healthy life. Noel Gallagher.' The Terence Higgins Trust later asks for the proceeds of the Earls Court gigs to go to charity. Despite a meeting between representatives of both parties Oasis do not accede to the request but agree to help otherwise.

They announce a replacement bassist on 18 September. He's Scott MacLeod, who was previously with Manchester band The Ya Yas. Record stores open at midnight on Sunday 1 October, to sell the first copies of (*What's the Story) morning glory?* At one stage Noel wanted to call the album *Flash in the pan*. Oasis turn up at London's Oxford Street Virgin megastore at midnight to play an acoustic set in front of 500 people, having spent most of the day in the pub watching a Liverpool v Man Utd game. Several hundred others are turned away (the gig had been announced on Greater London Radio that evening). They play: *Live forever, Wonderwall, She's electric, Round our way, Roll with it, Don't look back in anger, Hello* and *Cast no shadow*. Unfortunately, a drunken Liam has some problems remembering a lot of the lyrics to many of the songs. They stay until 3 a.m. signing autographs.

For the sleeve on the album Noel wanted an urban theme with something of a dark edge and a bit of mystique. He suggested Portobello Road in London in the morning but after four days driving around designer Brian Cannon came up with Berwick Street in Soho, because he thought there were a lot of interesting signs and buildings. The front sleeve shot was taken at 4.30 a.m. (the street lights are still glowing). It features two men passing each other by on the street, with one of them giving a knowing look. Towards the back of the shot on the left of the pavement there's a figure holding a white diamond-shaped object above his head. It's producer Owen Morris holding a master tape of the album. At the back of the

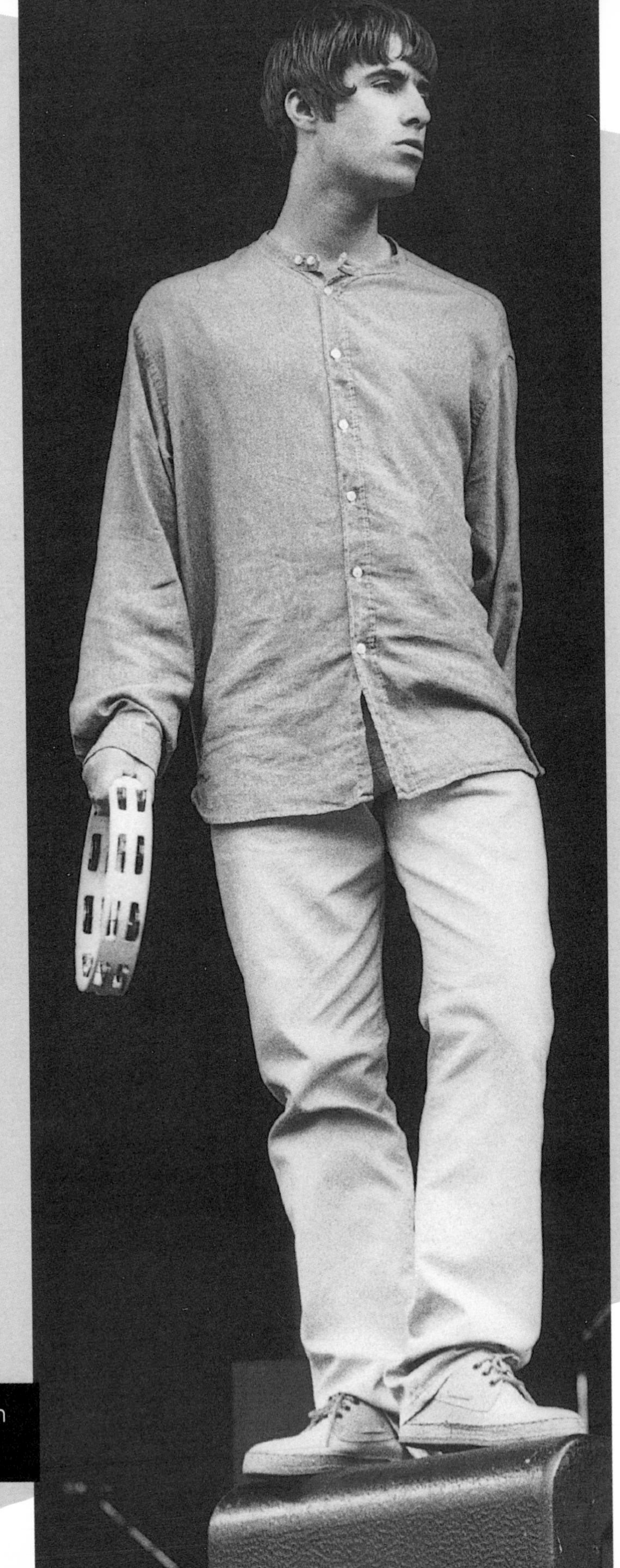

Mr Tambourine man: Liam at Slane (July 1995).

sleeve one of the streets crossing Berwick Street is ironically named 'Noel Street', but it can't be made out in the shot. The inside is meant to be like a classic cross between *Let it be* and *Revolver*.

As for the album itself the intro to *Hello* is actually a few riffs from *Wonderwall*. The message in the song is basically that it's good to be back making records after *Definitely maybe* and Noel even admits that it owes more than a debt to Gary Glitter (who gets a credit in the album as an excerpt is used from *Hello, hello I'm back again*). *Roll with it* is meant to be a message to people that you've just got to be yourself and get on with it, a similar sentiment expressed in *Supersonic*. Noel thinks it sounds like The Who while Alan McGee sees similarities with *Paperback writer*.

Wonderwall is about Noel's girlfriend, Meg Matthews, now with Creation Records. The title comes from the George Harrison album of the same name but the 'wonderwall' in Noel's life is Meg. He says he wrote it at a time when she was out of work and it is a song meant to cheer her up. *Backbeat* is also a reference to The Beatles and Noel reckons the drumming on it is the best Oasis have got on any song they've done. Bonehead plays piano on *Don't look back in anger* and it reminds Noel of a cross between *All the young dudes* and a couple of Beatles tracks. It's another song about looking forward to tomorrow and don't look back in anger at your life if anything has gone wrong, with a twist at the end of that maybe you can at some stage but not just now. The reference to standing beside the fireplace is when the three Gallagher brothers were made to pose for pictures every Christmas by their Mum to send a snapshot back home to their Gran in Ireland, while starting a revolution from the bed remark is a quote John Lennon once said (which he almost carried out with Yoko Ono during a famous nude sleep-in protest in a bed in Amsterdam in the early 70s). There is nobody known to them actually called Sally, it was just a name Noel came up with while in America.

Hey now is described by Noel as a cross between The Stone Roses' *I wanna be adored* and early Neil Young. It's about being in a group, looking back and admitting it has been hard work. Paul Weller plays harmonica on *The swamp song* and he and Noel play lead guitar. It's only 40 seconds but is eventually released on a longer version as a B-side to *Don't look back in anger* when it comes out as a single.

Some might say has a feel of it of The Faces or Slade. There are references to homeless people and about how people who can get what they want are moaning more than those who can't stay quiet. There's also trivial stuff about fishes and dishes purely for rhyming purposes. Tony McCarroll's drumming is kept on this track.

Cast no shadow is about Oasis's old mate, Richard Ashcroft, former singer with The Verve. It's about how Richard was always trying too hard but seemed to be living in the wrong place. One of the album's catchiest tracks, *She's electric*, is based on the children's TV programme from the 70s called *Stop, look and listen* with the chorus almost identical to this track. Liam wanted it to be the first single and Noel, while admitting it's a childish song, is coy as to whether it's a Blur pisstake. There's an *Apocalypse Now* touch to *Morning glory* with the helicopter noise at the beginning. It and *Champagne supernova* are meant as 'concept songs'. The mirror and razorblade refrain in *Morning glory* is an obvious reference to cocaine use and how some of the best ideas come when one is drugged out of it, only to forget them when the hit finishes. Noel describes the song as 'riot music' and about being parachuted into chaos. The title of the album is cryptically meant to be 'What is the story?' and Noel gives a clue by saying the songs are in order so that answer can be given in the last track.

Champagne supernova is meant to be psychedelic at the beginning before it turns into an epic rock tune. The getting high reference is not necessarily about drugs but can also mean about getting older. The landslide bit is about how Oasis have been caught at the bottom of one and there's loads of people piling up on top of them. Paul Weller provides lead guitar and backing vocals on this number.

One song which did not make it on to the album was *Step out*. Stevie Wonder had threatened litigation over a startling similarity to an old song of his called *Uptight*. *Step out* is omitted at the last minute, although it did make it on to initial promotional copies of the album. The controversial track eventually makes its appearance as a B-side to *Don't look back in anger*. Wonder joins the other original co-writers of *Uptight*, Sylvia Moy and Mark Cosy, as one of the credits alongside Noel for *Step out*.

At a party in London's Crossbar on 26 September Liam becomes involved in an altercation with a drunk at the bar who hits him. Liam retaliates. The DJ puts on *Roll with it* and both Liam and Noel leave. The following day's *Daily Star* splashes across its front page the 'news' – 'Top of the dopes: Pop idols' drug shock' – in reference to explicit lyrics on the new album, particularly on *Morning glory* and *Champagne supernova*. Noel would later joke about that story: 'Oasis in drugs shock? It's no shock to us!'

The *Daily Star* article had been based on an interview in the upcoming issue of *The Face* magazine written by Ashley Heath. Noel admits: 'I put drug references in Oasis songs because I take them and I write about what I know. Me and my mates have been doing drugs since we were 14.' He adds he wanted Liam to write lyrics at some stage but when he did produce one song called *Alice* its lyrics were 'pathetic, just cheesy, horrible, scally boy stuff'. In the same piece Liam says he fancies Donna from Elastica. The singer, who's reputedly been linked to at least 50 women, says, 'I just get out there and get on with it. I'll have sex wherever.' Bonehead remarks: 'If he has got a different girl in his bed every night I don't ever see them.'

The 30 September issue of *Melody Maker* carries a lukewarm review of the album by David Stubbs. It doesn't even rate on their star-billing system as 'bloody essential' or 'recommended'. Stubbs says the new release is 'occasionally sublime but too often laboured and lazy. On this evidence Oasis are a limited band.' Amazingly, he even says *Don't look back in anger* 'disappoints too', while *Champagne supernova* 'ends up sounding merely hollow'!

But in the November issue of *Select* the album receives a more positive review from Andrew Harrison

who gives it a mark of four out of five. '*Morning glory* is a great album, just not quite as great as the last one,' he comments. 'But when Noel makes his *Rubber soul,* it won't be for trying too hard.'

Noel reveals that he was forced to leave a Take That concert (of all things) early with Meg after dozens of teenybopper fans turned their hatred on him when Howard Donald announced from the stage that they'd like to convey their best wishes to Robbie Williams 'as long as he doesn't join Oasis'. Williams had hung out with Oasis backstage at Glastonbury and pictures of him in a drunken and generally dishevelled state there appalled his management and the other squeaky clean boys, ultimately leading to him to being sacked from the band (for that 'crime' among other reasons). Williams's association with Oasis gets so hyped that on a number of occasions in the tabloid press it's hinted he may replace Liam as singer with the band at some future date!

Noel admits he was told it was 'time to leave' by an usher at Wembley Arena in a bid to get away from the baying Take That fans. He says he has been on the terraces at Millwall, Chelsea, Manchester United and Leeds 'and yet this was the most terrifying experience I've ever had'! He also opens up on Oasis's drug habit again: 'Nobody in Oasis has ever done heroin, crack, acid or any form of downers or anything that makes you lose the marbles big time. Most of the band get stoned, we all get pissed, we all do E every now and again. We're not as mad as people make us out to be . . . regardless of what anybody might think, Oasis has never, ever gone onstage high or drunk.' As for the plagiarism allegations levelled against him: 'When I hear the first record that rips off one of my songs I'll find the guy, I'll shake him by the hand, I'll make sure my publishing company sues no one.' He also hints again that Oasis will take a long break after their third album, for which he says he already has the ideas for title, sleeve cover and running order. While they may reconvene in 1998 he sees Oasis as a long-term project until at least 2000.

(*What's the story*) *morning glory?* goes straight into the UK and Irish charts at No 1, selling a staggering 350,000 copies in just two days in Britain and an additional

250,000 copies in the US. It's the fastest-selling album since Michael Jackson's 1987 album *Bad*. By the end of May 1995 *Morning glory* will have sold nearly three million copies in the UK and a further two million in America – it's predicted it could eventually top 15 million sales worldwide.

Noel says in a radio interview: 'Being in Oasis is not a bowl of cherries . . . we've had our ups and downs. This year we've had more downs than ups, and that's probably reflected in the album. That's a document of being in Oasis in late '94 – '95.' As to some mixed reviews, he adds: 'I don't care what people say about the album – that it's not as good as *Definitely maybe*, or it's too ballady or it's too deep . . . I'm not bothered. It's a batch of songs that I wrote and lyrics that I wrote at the time.'

The show at Bournemouth International Centre gets a cool response from reviewer Richard Smith in the 14 October issue of *Melody Maker*. 'Oasis weren't that good,' he confesses. 'Sure there were times they soared . . . but other times they just lacked lust . . . I bet even God has bad days.' The gig at Stoke-on-Trent's Trentham Gardens is more enthusiastically received by Andy Richardson in the *NME* edition of the same date. 'No intricacy or clever-cleverness here, just honest, dynamic, straightforward rock 'n' roll,' he says.

On 17 October the band are hit by the shock departure of Scott McLeod while they're in the middle of a North American tour in Buffalo, New York. The reasons appear to be that he's homesick, feels he doesn't fit in and is having problems coping with large crowds. The group is forced to cancel some US and Canadian dates in Toronto, Detroit and Chicago. Oasis also have to appear on the *David Letterman Show* as a four-piece with Bonehead on bass – they play *Morning glory* and are delighted to meet William Shatner, who played Captain Kirk in *Star Trek*, backstage. They fly back to Britain on 20 October. 'What happened was we did a gig in Pittsburgh and he [*Scott*] comes off stage and goes straight to bed on the tour bus,' Noel tells Radio 1. 'The tour manager had this really strange face on him. He says, "Oh, Scott has decided he wants to go home." So we all decided we were going to let him sleep on it and if he got up in the morning and changed his mind, fair enough. But by the time we got up he was on the plane home. The funny thing is he didn't speak to me personally about it. I got back from America when we did the Letterman show and he phoned up, believe it or not, and he says, "All right, it's Scott." And I said, "What do you want?" and he's actually changed his mind and says he thinks he's made the wrong decision. And I said, "I think you have, good luck with signing on."'

Scott, who's believed to be joining a new band called Saint Jack, explains to the *Manchester Evening News*: 'I compared the two bands and preferred Saint Jack. I had a feeling that this was a good band. At the end of the day, that is why I wanted to come back.'

Guigsy makes a miraculous recovery and rejoins the band at a rehearsal on 26 October. Despite being told by a doctor to take six months off he feels he's ready for action again and the goings-on with Scott may have been an added spur. Full steam ahead again.

Paul Weller tells the December issue of *Q*: 'I like Noel's songs. It's an obvious thing, but he's a fucking good writer. And whether the knives are drawn for him now or not doesn't matter, 'cos he's got it. He'll just get better and better. There are some great songs on the new LP – *Don't look back in anger* is a classic.' Asked is he worried about Noel's substance abuse, given that Noel claimed recently (and subsequently denies) that he snorts a line of coke every 40 minutes, Weller says: 'Sometimes – but he's taking the piss with quotes like that. Whenever I see Noel, he's quite together. I've only seen him frothing at the mouth once. A lot of that's bullshit.'

As Noel himself points out: 'I take cocaine, big fucking deal. It's a social thing and I've been doing it since before I was even in a band . . . in fact, I wish I'd never started smoking cigarettes or drinking beer or taking cocaine or ecstasy because I'd have a lot more money than I do have.'

For a man worth a reputed £7.5 million has no reason to look back in anger.

Wonderful Wonderwall

A significant date in Oasis's history is 30 October. Today they release *Wonderwall*. The track may only go on to reach No 3 but it's the song that propels Oasis to super-stardom in Britain, blaring out of every radio almost every hour of the day. It's a 1990s classic, the favourite song of the year for millions, played by buskers everywhere, a soon-to-be party piece for thousands this coming Christmas, a treasure for fans and my own personal best-loved Oasis track.

The single is accompanied by the poppish *Round are way*, the eight-minute-long instrumental *The swamp song*, which they are now inclined to open shows with since Glastonbury, and the epic *The masterplan*, featuring strings, brass and Noel's vocals and which he describes as 'the best song I've ever written'. All three B-sides were recorded at Maison Rouge in September. The circus-feel video for the single was shot predominantly in black and white at Woolwich. Many fans think the girl on the sleeve to *Wonderwall* is Noel's girlfriend, Meg Matthews, but designer Brian Cannon kindly informs me it is in fact Anita Heryet, a Creation employee. It's Brian's arm holding out the mirror.

In a rare interview just after they play *Wonderwall* on *Top of the Pops*, Guigsy admits it's good to be back with the band. 'The doctor's given me loads of pills, so that should help,' he says. 'The worst thing is I've been told to eat loads of vegetables to keep my strength up, and I hate vegetables.' *Wonderwall* goes straight into the charts at No 3, held off by Robson and Jerome's *I believe* and Coolio's *Gangsta's paradise*.

NME's John Robinson describes *Wonderwall* in the 28 October edition as one of Oasis's best records but says the really pleasant surprise is *Round are way*. 'The mood is *Our house* by Madness but with better vocals, heavier guitars and a brass section nicked from The Boo Radleys, which nearly makes it a *Penny Lane* for the 90s,' he observes.

The mammoth Earls Court gigs arrive on 4 and 5 November. Two giant posters of Liam and Noel adorn either side of the entrance to the arena. They were taken by Jill Furmanovsky at their gig in Sheffield. They'll later turn up on display by the A40 in London just before Christmas and in February '96 they are hung from Chelsea bridge (they are soon blown down in a storm and ripped to shreds).

The inside of the venue is curtained off for sound and effect reasons. The Bootleg Beatles provide support. Each night Oasis kick off to 20,000 fans with *The swamp song*, quickly followed by *Acquiesce* and on the second night they're joined by The Bootleg Beatles for *I am the walrus*. The gigs are an enormous success and get a huge thumbs-up from reviewer Paul Moody in *NME* on 18 November under a piece titled 'The stardust brothers'. Enthusing about *Cigarettes and alcohol* and *Champagne supernova* he points out: 'They may have the capacity to backfire at will and possess the onstage demeanour of a group permanently caught in the rigor mortis of a sound-check, but Earls Court proved that, among other things, Oasis have got the trust and belief of the nation in their hands like no other group in the country.' *Select's* Ian Harrison says: 'We file out, touched by something sublime. It's like a world-class gig from antiquity that Fluff Freeman could have enjoyed.'

At the aftershow parties there's an unprecedented celebrity count with among those showing up Elton John, Paula Yates, Robbie Williams, Michael Hutchence, George Michael, Alex 'Hurricane' Higgins, members of U2 and the Pet Shop Boys' Neil Tennant. Noel presents the Bootleg Beatles with a case of champagne and tells them it's the next best thing to the real thing – The Beatles – having them play that weekend.

Noel presents the other four members of the band with scooters he bought in London. Both Noel and Liam turn up to the annual *Q* magazine awards at London's

Park Lane Hotel on 7 November. Oasis pick up the award for Best Live Act. Ronnie Wood presents the award with Noel joking on acceptance, 'I'll accept this award on behalf of a crap album with crap lyrics.' Blur win the Best Album for the second year in succession.

They take off for some more dates in America where *Wonderwall* has gone straight into the US charts at No 21 (it will eventually rise as high as No 5 there by March) and *(What's the story) morning glory?* has sold over one million copies Stateside (it will top over two million by the spring). Liam tells US magazine *Alternative Press* that he has a feeling he won't live till the age of 40. 'Some nights I'm on the verge of blackout. When I get to 25 or 30 the heart attack will be kicking in.'

Noel also clears up some confusion about their plans after the third album. He explains; 'I said that after the third album maybe we were gonna take quite a bit of time off because we put out records every three months and an album every year. So maybe people want a rest. Of course, I'm not gonna take any time off now 'cos I'm starting to write an album as soon as we get off tour. Just maybe step back from the media machine for a while.'

On 28 November they record a *Later with Jools Holland* session for broadcast on 31 December. They record three songs, Slade's *Cum on feel the noize*, *Wonderwall* and a medley of *Round are way* and *Up in the sky*. Noel and Liam duet on the first and Noel takes the lead vocals on the rest. But the producers are unhappy with Liam's performance and unusually do a retake with just Noel on vocals on the first track. The excuse is Liam has been up for three days and has got the flu. The broadcast goes out without him.

Noel shows up at Brixton Academy on 29 and 30 November to support Paul Weller by playing an acoustic set of *Wonderwall*, *Talk tonight*, *Whatever*, *Cast no shadow*, *Don't look back in anger* plus a cover of The Beatles, *You've got to hide your love away*. The band also go into the studio to record a version of *You've got to hide your love away* for Radio 1 to be broadcast on the Chris Evans show on 1 December, World Aids Day. Noel announces Oasis will not release an album in 1996 and will concentrate on America instead.

Liam meets up with Damon backstage at the MTV awards in Paris and goes up to his dressing-room to apologise over Noel's AIDS comments. 'Sorry for what our kid said, it was out of order,' he stutters. 'He's a twat. I still think your album's shit though.' Damon replies: 'And yours is too!' The two apparently sit down together and Liam says Oasis and Blur should always hate each other and there should always be rivalry because 'that's rock 'n' roll'. They part on good terms.

Noel tells Manchester radio station Key 103 that he hates writing lyrics. 'It really bugs me,' he says. 'We need a Morrissey in the band, but he's too fat.'

Elastica's Justine Frischmann, Damon Albarn's girlfriend, finally breaks her silence about Liam. He had made his amorous intentions toward her quite crudely known in the past and at the MTV awards apparently told

Damon, 'How's your missus? Tell her to leave the back door open as usual.' When asked by Sydney music paper *The Dram Media* to free-associate the word Oasis she responded, 'Hamster'. She explains: 'You know, Liam having the brain of a hamster and all that. A brain the size of hamster's brain, that's all, not the entire hamster.'

Oasis become involved in an anti-drugs video by the parents of tragic ecstasy victim Leah Betts. *Wonderwall* was played at her funeral. The song is used in a video reconstruction of her last hours.

Wonderwall is also covered as an easy listening tune with a 50s feel by The Mike Flowers Pops. 'When I first heard that someone had done a cover of *Wonderwall*, it was like, "Who?"', Noel recalls. 'Someone said it was this guy Mike Flowers Pops. I said I'd never heard of him but when we got the tape we fell about in hysterics, but not in a derogatory way. Everybody in the band thinks it's great. *Wonderwall* is a song, a great song the way we do it, but he's changed all the chords around and he's kept the same melody and that's the sign of a great, great song. I mean, I'd like to hear anyone doing a Nine Inch Nails cover. Good luck to the guy and I really mean that.'

Mike Flowers says: 'Noel showed up to one of my gigs in London and although I did not meet him personally I believe he likes my version.' Ironically, the Mike Flowers version of *Wonderwall* goes to No 2 in the charts, one place higher than Oasis had obtained. It is beaten to be the Christmas No 1 by Michael Jackson's *Earth Song*.

(*What's the story*) *morning glory?* only makes it to the No 3 spot in the critics' awards of the year in the Christmas issue of *Melody Maker*. Pulp's *Different class* pulls off the No 1 slot with Tricky's *Maxinquayr* coming in second (Blur's *The great escape* is 10th). Pulp also win Single of the Year with *Common people* with Supergrass' *Alright* at No 2. *Some might say* is No 3, *Wonderwall* No 6. Oddly, after all the Blur versus Oasis fuss in the summer, neither *Roll with it* nor *Country house* registers in the top 50, with Blur's only chart placing at No 23 for *The universal*.

Back home in Manchester for the holidays Noel, Liam and Guigsy turn up at a Manchester City home game against Chelsea and are brought on to the pitch to be introduced to the crowd. Noel takes a shot at goals but hits the post. It had been rumoured that Oasis may sponsor Man City's jerseys but nothing concrete has ever come of it.

On 21 December former drummer Tony McCarroll issues a High Court writ for unfair dismissal, seeking compensation. The case will be heard in the New Year.

It's Christmas time and Creation decide to throw a party at London's Halcyon Hotel on 22 December to celebrate an amazing year. Alan McGee has a few tricks up his sleeve and around midnight he stands up and asks for quiet while he announces he has a few presents for the Oasis boys. There are only four boxes, though. He hands Alan White a large wrapped box. When he opens it there is a toy Mini Cooper with a Union Jack on its roof which puzzles the drummer. Then McGee hands Alan a Christmas card. He opens it and inside is a cheque which covers the cost of a Mini Cooper. Alan is naturally taken aback. Bonehead is handed a Rolex watch and a Christmas card. The card tells him there's a brand new piano waiting for him back in his living-room in Manchester. Guigsy is also presented with a Rolex and membership of a gym while Liam is then called over. He gets a Rolex too, a box of clothes and a Gibson Epiphone guitar, a copy of one which John Lennon used to use. Liam has recently started to learn the guitar.

Noel is secretly puzzled as to why there are no boxes for him and thinks he's been short-changed. But McGee tells him to follow him outside. He agrees. Outside a brown Rolls-Royce Corniche is parked in the driveway and McGee points to it. Noel goes, 'What?' Alan: 'It's yours!' Noel: 'No way, it's not – that Rolls-Royce!' Alan: 'It is!' Noel: 'But what am I supposed to do with it? I can't drive!' Alan: 'Well, I don't know.' Noel had always said he wanted a Rolls-Royce if the band ever 'made it'. Brown is his favourite colour. Alan McGee thought to himself that Noel and Oasis had saved his record company by selling six million records. So why not give the guy what he wants as a rock 'n' roll gesture. Noel still can't drive and is chauffeured around in the car on special occasions by his mate, Simon. Oasis's Christmas 1995 certainly ended in a wonderhaul!

Hat Trick at the Brits

Oasis kick off 1996 with a string of nominations in *NME*'s Brat awards. They're up for best band, best album and best single (*Wonderwall* and *Some might say* – voted by *NME* readers), best live act, best video (*Live by the sea*). Tricky's *Maxinquayr* picks up the critics' award for best album while Black Grape's *Reverend black grape* wins best single.

Liam spent part of the New Year in Dublin with his new girlfriend, Patsy Kensit. They had also been spotted at Manchester's Victoria and Albert Hotel over the Christmas. She has split from her long-time husband, Jim Kerr of Simple Minds. Patsy and Kerr shared a house in the upmarket Dublin suburb of Killiney, next door to the likes of Bono, Chris de Burgh and Enya. It's believed she may have been introduced to Liam by Robbie Williams. Liam books into the Berkeley Court Hotel as 'John F. Kennedy', Patsy as 'Mary Robinson' (the Irish President).

All seven of their singles are in the top 75 over the festive period and rumours increase about a possible show at Balloch Castle country park on the banks of Loch Lomond in Scotland. There had already been whispers of possible shows at Manchester's Maine Road and London's Wembley Stadium.

It's also officially announced that Tony McCarroll is seeking damages from the band as well as royalties from *(What's the story?) morning glory*. A High Court writ issued on his behalf, brought on 5 January by McCarroll's solicitors, Jens Hills, reads: 'His expulsion from Oasis was due to Noel Gallagher's personal dislike of him and had nothing to do with his abilities as a musician.' It further emerges that McCarroll was told formally he was no longer required to drum with Oasis by the band's manager Marcus Russell on behalf of Oasis on 28 April 1995. Tony had a phone conversation with Bonehead that evening. The writ had originally been issued on 21 December against Noel, Liam, Guigsy and Alan. It says that Oasis signed a contract with Sony Music Entertainment (UK) Limited on 22 October 1993. The five members agreed to record up to five albums for the label. At the time Noel asked Tony not to sign a deal with Sony and instead sign a separate deal as a session musician. McCarroll claims the dismissal effectively dissolves the original management deal involving the five founding members of Oasis. He is seeking a declaration that he was unlawfully fired, compensation and costs as well as demanding accounts, a declaration that the original Oasis partnership involving his name is dissolved and an order that the partnership be wound up.

Meanwhile, Noel insists his battle with Blur is 'finished ... all over' and confidently predicts Oasis will 'clean up' at the forthcoming Brit awards. Oasis had been asked to play at them but turned down the offer saying they'd rather party the night away.

The British tabloid press target Liam big time as a 'bad boy'. The 14 January issue of the *News of the World* carries a story titled 'Oasis rat Liam loo-ved me and left me'. Singer Berri, who had hits with *Sunshine after the rain* and *Shine like a star*, claims she rescued Liam from a pack of groupies, he offered to take her to the south of France and they had 'passionate' sex in the toilets. She describes him as 'very naughty and very adventurous' and gives him a rating of 'ten out of ten'. She is reported 'heartbroken' when Liam leaves the hotel that night with a mystery blonde.

The 15 January issue of the *Sun* carries another wacky tale about Liam's past at a car valet service when he was younger. It claims he once threw a bucket of water over Ryan Giggs, scratched Eric Cantona's Audi and rubbed wire-wool on Paul Ince's BMX. The allegations had already become a bit of an urban myth in Manchester but my own investigations through the Gallagher family ties show that no such incidents ever took place.

Later the same day Noel has his first outing in his Rolls-Royce when he and Meg are driven to the launch

Liam spots some rock dinosaur called Bono!

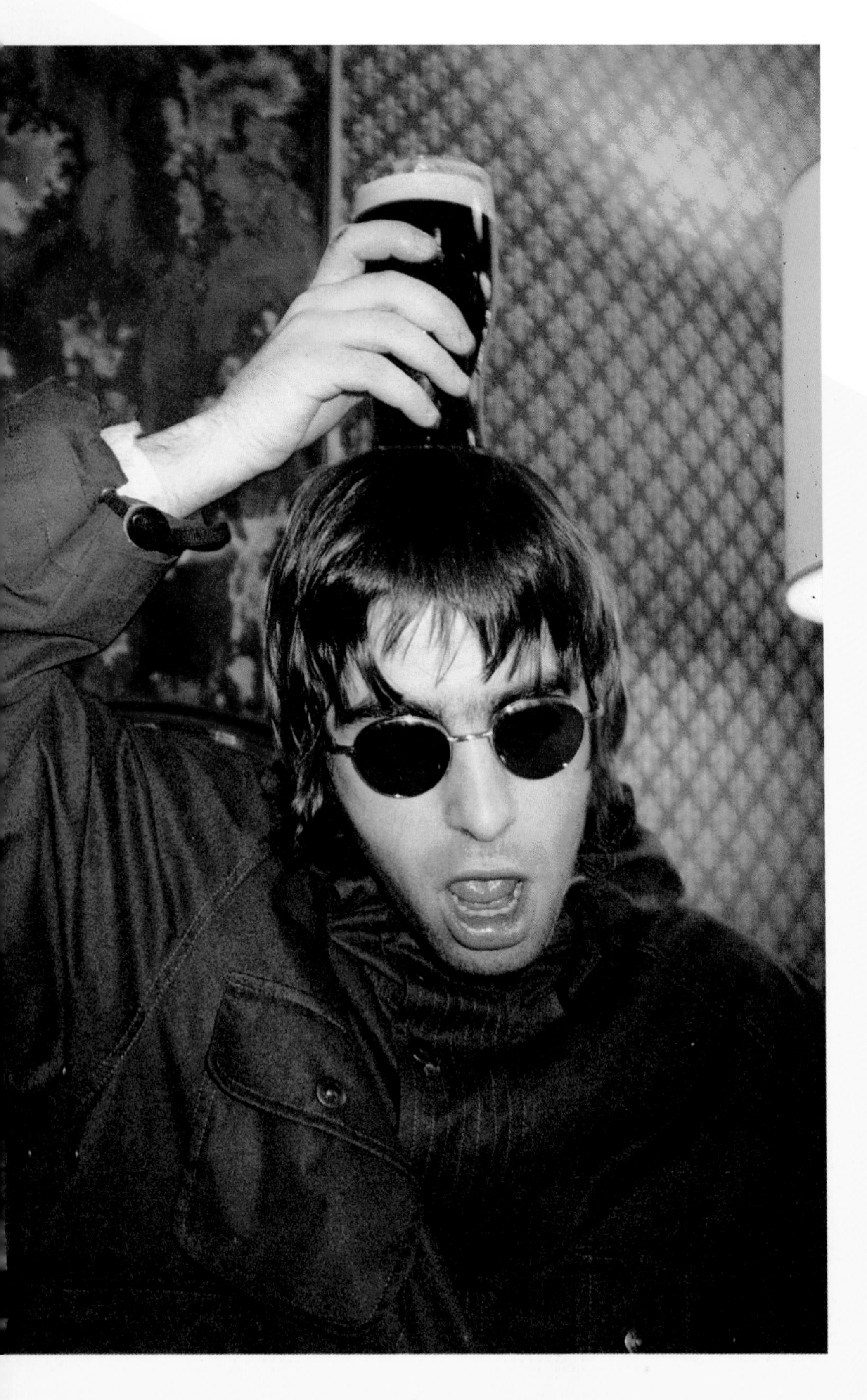

of the Brit awards at London's Hard Rock Cafe where, upon his arrival, he's immediately the centre of press attention.

The tabloids soon get a hold of Liam's dalliance with Patsy Kensit. The *News of the World* on 21 January claims Liam is 'two-timing' Patsy with a sexy French singer, Sandrine de la Plage. She too claims Liam offered her a French holiday and that she went to his room where he turned out to be 'a total flop in bed'. She 'cried all the way home' when Liam refused to see her again. Liam tells the following day's *Sun* that Patsy is 'a top girl and we enjoy being together . . . we're both perfect for each other, we both love getting out of our heads'. Liam refers to the kiss-and-tell stories in the 2 May issue of *Rolling Stone*, an interview conducted in February: 'Women have had me over. It's happened twice in the last month. After I've bopped 'em, they've gone and sold it to the papers and made money out of it. Fair play. But I've just come in their gob and gone off, so therefore I've had them over. Tied one-all, baby.'

Don't look back in anger, the intro for which bears a startling resemblance to John Lennon's *Imagine*, is due for release as a single on 19 February, avoiding a clash with Blur's *Stereotypes* which is released a week later. The video for the new Oasis release is shot in Los Angeles at a mansion in Beverly Hills and stars Patrick McNee, who used to play Steed in *The Avengers* and *New Avengers*. While the appearance of a black London taxi may give the impression it's shot in England the video is indeed made in LA during Oasis's American tour.

Two new Oasis covers bands crop up in Scotland. One is called The Gallaghers and the other No Way Sis. Both Liam and Noel turned up to one of The Gallaghers' shows in Edinburgh but the band does not last too long and No Way Sis, with convincing Liam and Noel lookalikes, emerge as the more long-term professional copycat act. Noel will later catch the band at London's Forum.

It's 23 January and it's up to Noel alone to represent Oasis at the *NME* Brat awards. Bonehead is at home in Manchester celebrating his daughter Lucy's first birthday while Alan White is messing with his new car. Noel tells MTV that Guigsy is chilling out somewhere 'with a big fat spliff' and 'our kid' [*Liam*] has 'allegedly' been seen in an Edinburgh bar. 'Come home,' he winks, 'all is forgiven.' During the presentations the only occasions when Noel rises to his feet are when Paul Weller gets the award for Best Solo Artist, Michael Eavis (the organiser of Glastonbury, which is called off until 1997) gets the 'Godlike Genius' award and Go! Discs' Tony Crean receives a special award for organising the *Help* album. But soon Noel walks up to the podium to collect no less than four awards for Best Live Act, Best Single (*Wonderwall*), Best Album and Best Band. 'It's hard to be humble at times like this so I won't try – you're all shit,' he jokes.

INXS singer Michael Hutchence is also at the Brats and is quoted as saying that his next album will 'piss all over anything that Noel Gallagher has done'. An enraged Noel gets to hear of this and later says, 'Anyone who wants to pick a fight with me is gonna fuckin' get one.' Noel and Meg are later pictured celebrating the awards outside the venue with Meg leaning backwards over the bonnet of the Rolls-Royce.

On 3 February Liam and Patsy make their first public appearance together at the Supermodels' fashion show in Dublin's The Point. Liam takes a front-row seat alongside Patsy beside the catwalk. Pictures of them kissing and caressing appear in the following Monday's papers. He scarpers backstage after a few minutes and watches the event on his own on a TV monitor in the bar. He goes back to his hotel and his plane ticket, left in Irish publicist Justin Green's car, is later sent round by courier.

Tickets go on sale at 9 a.m. on 9 February for Oasis's homecoming gig at Maine Road in Manchester, home of their heroes, Manchester City. The capacity will be increased from 35,000 to 39,000 for the Oasis show and will be their biggest gig ever. Tickets sell out in three hours, with queues in Manchester forming as early as 5 a.m. Due to demand they add another date within weeks. A rumoured 13 July concert at Wembley Stadium does not materialise with a show at Knebworth now the preferred option.

Noel appears on the cover of February's *Q* with the headline 'Noel Gallagher: the greatest songwriter of the '90s'. 'When I'm writing a song, that's it, I'll sit up in this chair 48 hours, smoking, drinking, playing the same line all over again,' he tells Phil Sutcliffe. 'I put that girl [*Meg*] through hell. When I'm going through all that, them chaps [*the other members of the band*] are in their cosy beds, with their cosy lives – it's all cosy for them. Actually the big dream is to be U2 – not a little Britpop phenomenon with the right clothes and trendy haircuts, which is what we are now.'

The 10 February issue of *Melody Maker* carries the first review of *Don't look back in anger*. They get praise from The Stud brothers for putting on decent tracks as B-sides. 'From its *Imagine* intro to its storming conclusion this is, as we already know, a very good song indeed,' they concur.

Noel appears on the cover of the 17 February issue of *NME*. He's basking in the glory of the Brat awards and chuffed the album has done so well despite mixed reviews when it first came out. He's also thrilled that *Wonderwall* is shooting up the American charts where it has gone to No 5. 'If you took a kid from the Bronx and a kid from Brixton who probably have nothing in common whatsoever, the one thing they'd have in common is they'd own a copy of *Morning glory*,' he ponders. 'That's something to be proud of.'

As the new album was written mainly on acoustic guitar and he's now got his own amp he predicts any new releases might be a bit of a cross between the two albums and may be more experimental in sound. The same issue of *NME* carries a review of *Don't look back in anger* by Ted Kessler. He points out that as Liam is not singing on the release it's 'a bit like Newcastle without Ferdinand, full of Noel's Beardsley-esque artistry but lacking Liam's thrilling, free-scoring attack'. He rates *Underneath the sky* as even better than the single.

The band score their second No 1 single when *Don't look back in anger* shoots straight into the UK charts at No 1 on 18 February. It's backed by *Step out*, *Underneath the sky* and a cover of Slade's *Cum on feel the noize*. The sleeve to the single actually cost more to make than a normal album cover. It took three days to shoot in a west London studio with photographer Michael Spencer

Jones. A white piano was hired for the picture but all the rest of the instruments belong to the band. The idea was inspired by an incident with Ringo Starr during the 60s when he disappeared for a while during the recording of *The white album*. After pleas to return he arrived back to find his drum kit covered in carnations. Oasis flew in

Patsy Kensit and Liam at a fashion show in Dublin.

10,000 white and red carnations from Colombia (no, that was the only commodity in the consignment!) for the shoot. Two thousand were sent off to Holland to be dyed blue and flown back again. Designer Brian Cannon says he managed to save some of the carnations for his mother but it broke his heart to dump the rest in a skip.

Oasis's triumph at the Brit awards on 19 February at Earls Court is usurped somewhat by the antics of Jarvis Cocker. During Michael Jackson's over-the-top performance of *Earth song* he clambers up onstage and starts jumping around, pulling faces and generally causing a disruption while Jacko is hoisted aloft overhead by a crane. It's alleged that Jarvis caused injury to two children, is arrested, bailed, but later vindicated. Oasis win three awards on the night. It does not quite match Blur's record four awards at last year's Brits but the band are thrilled. (Blur, incidentally, do not show up at the '96 awards.)

Their first award of the night is for *Wonderwall* as Best Video, as voted by viewers of ITV's *The Chart Show*. INXS singer Michael Hutchence is meant to present the award to Oasis. Patsy Kensit had been pictured backstage at the MTV awards jokingly putting her hand down Hutchence's trousers while Liam has made several bitchy remarks about Paula Yates, Hutchence's girlfriend. A newly bearded Liam saunters up and says: 'I heard Michael's going to give me a slap around the face. So come on . . .' Hutchence instead kisses him. Liam responds by saying, 'I'd just like to say . . .' before Noel interrupts and blurts, 'Sausages!' (This is believed to be a reference to Liam's prominent role in a recent 'sausage' boardgame-type send-up in the *Sun* about celebrities' intertwined sex lives.) Noel says, 'Has-beens shouldn't be presenting fucking awards to gonna-bes' and adds, 'I am extremely rich and you [*the audience/reviewers*] are not.' The attack, like most of Oasis's four-letter diatribes at the Brits, are edited from the following evening's TV broadcast. Guigsy later had an altercation with Hutchence at a backstage party after the Australian kept poking him in the shoulder.

Noel later explains that the arrogant 'I'm rich and you're not' remark was not aimed at the general public. He had spotted a 'cheeky twat' near the front of the audience wearing a Blur top who had been getting on his wick all night with his attitude and directed the comment directly at him.

Noel also appreciates the fact that the video award is voted for by the public and not by industry bigwigs like most of the Brits. He says onstage: 'Anything that's voted for by the fans is special. Anything that's voted for by idiots, corporate pigs, means nothing to us . . . they can take their awards and stick them right up their country houses.' He later says: 'We need the people of England who are on the dole, unemployed and who buy the records to tell us how good we are. That's all that matters.'

Lenny Kravitz presents their second award of the night for Best Album for *(What's the story) morning glory?* All TV viewers see is Liam saying, 'I'd like to thank . . . all the people' before a clip of *Don't look back in anger* is shown. But onstage Liam mouths off: 'Anyone tough enough to take us off the stage can come up now. It will take more than ginger bollocks (*host Chris Evans*) to throw us off.' He then starts singing, 'All the people, so many people' to the air of Blur's *Parklife* before the rest of the band join in by singing 'They go hand in hand, hand in hand, through their shite-life'. Liam next pretends to ram the award up his bottom and then sniffs the end of the statuette.

Pete Townsend presents their third and final award of the night for Best British Group. Noel praises Alan McGee and Labour leader Tony Blair, who is in attendance to present an award to David Bowie, and he appeals to viewers to vote Labour in the next general election before ending with the slogan, 'Power to the people!' They return to their table, where all their girlfriends, including Patsy Kensit, are seated, and down a few more cratefuls of beer.

Wonderwall loses out as best single to *Back for good* by Take That, who make their final public appearance in Britain together as they are splitting up.

Noel later tells the press conference when asked if he has any message for Blur: 'Yes, goodbye. Pack your bags now because you're finished. You've had a *Parklife* and now it's a "Shitelife" for you.' He complains about why the likes of a 'weather girl' should be presenting an award and not the likes of Paul Weller, Paul McCartney or Keith Richards. He also complains that Annie Lennox shouldn't get an award at the expense of Bjork or PJ Harvey while Michael Jackson is there only 'to further his own career' and Simply Red's Mick Hucknall is a 'fat idiot'. He soon turns on the general establishment for some bizarre reason. 'Behead all Tories and the Royal Family,' he cries. 'Vote Labour.' He praises Jarvis for his stage invasion but complains 'he should've fuckin' headbutted the c*** [*Jacko*] . . . people hate c***s like him, Annie Lennox and Phil Collins.'

Guigsy and Bonehead stay on for a while at the after-show party while the rest of the band, accompanied by Robbie Williams, Lisa Moorish, Vic Reeves and various record company personnel, retire back to Marylebone Hotel.

The next day's early editions of the papers announce Oasis's night of glory to their readers. 'Wonderhaul', proclaims the *Sun*. 'Oasis are different class', heralds the *Daily Mirror*, 'Oasis are the beast of Brits', says the *Daily Star*, in reference not only to their win but their onstage behaviour.

Liam shows an unusual trait of arrogant misogynism when he's interviewed by Ken Midcaliff for the March issue of *Sky* magazine. The interview was done just before the Brits in a bar just across the road from Creation's headquarters in London. The singer toys with a pretty red-haired waitress and pesters her for her phone number. She finally relents. Liam looks at it, smiles, crumples it up and throws it away. 'Birds are all right,' he says. 'They're all pink on the inside. Any bird who's fit is all right, unless she's nicked or ugly and she speaks backwards to you. If she thinks I'm boss, then thumbs up. Chicks in Japan don't even ask your name, just "Can I sleep with you tonight?" Certainly, my dear. I like American birds till they open their mouths. Then they annoy me. But if they're fit, they're fit.'

As to The Beatles similarities, Noel explains: 'It's always intentional. I'm always trying to rip The Beatles off for anything and everything. People always say, "Don't you want to be innovative?" Well, no. We just want to make good records . . . whenever I start feeling good about myself, I just think of The Beatles' albums and those eight years, and I know I ain't that fucking good, not yet. But I will be that good.' Most of his fans would already agree that Noel is well on his way to achieving that burning ambition.

America Calls But Noel Cops It Back Home

America beckons for Oasis. Despite losing the battle to Blur in the summer singles charts they're now firmly established as the kingpins of Britpop, the biggest British band of the 90s, and can leave petty squabbles with Blur behind them as they now outsell them at home by three to one. There's virgin territory waiting to be conquered. The night before they fly out to New York they copper-fasten their stranglehold on the British music scene by making history on *Top of the Pops* – they're the first band in 15 years to perform two songs on the same night on the old lady of TV pop (The Beatles and The Jam being the only other two groups to pull off the same achievement). Noel, who for the first time in public is brandishing his Union Jack guitar which girlfriend Meg gave him for Christmas, has his little jibe again at Blur (who're also in the studio) when he announces at the start of the show: 'Best band in the world, live and exclusive, and it's not Blur.' They play *Don't look back in anger* and a cover of Slade's *Cum on feel the noize*.

They arrive in America on 22 February, the same day as the *Top of the Pops* recording is due to be broadcast, for their seventh tour of the States. Even the high-brow Channel 4 News is taking an interest in Oasis's impact on America and despatches a crew to monitor their progress. What they find is another British band, Bush, are filling out huge 20,000-seater stadia as they capitalise on the Pearl Jam grunge-type market, even though they're relatively unknown back home. Oasis, on the other hand, are still playing club-size venues, although they're now selling out in most places as word of mouth feedback and heavy rotation of *Wonderwall* on the airwaves engrains itself on American youth's subconsciousness. (*What's the story?*) *morning glory* has spent three weeks at No 5 in the Billboard album chart. It's already a number one album in Britain, Ireland, Australia and is in the top ten in ten European countries. *Wonderwall* will reach a high of No 5 in the singles chart during their trip to America. The only problem Oasis have in America is their accents – at one stage an MTV interview is subtitled so viewers can understand the Manc dialect!

Even Courtney Love is getting worried. The Hole singer reputedly posts the following message on the internet (it's not known if it's meant to be a wisecrack): 'Oasis must die. Do not buy Oasis records. They will come to rape our women and invade America.'

During some of the more low-key American dates Noel premieres drafts of a couple of new songs. One is titled *My big mouth*, which as the name suggests is about his motormouth and how he could fly a plane in it it's so big. It is a rock 'n' roll song with a Stranglers-like bass line. The other track is a heartfelt love song with a catchy melody tentatively titled *Setting sun*. He's also believed to have another new song up his sleeve called *New suede shoes*.

NME covers the start of the tour in Kansas City and Andy Richardson reports that 'the Kansas gig is impressive enough; Liam Gallagher's voice tougher than ever, Noel's now customary acoustic slot cool and passionate, and their slow-ending version of *I am the walrus* is monumental.' But he also notes that the fans remain passionless and Oasis 'leave with a measure of disappointment'. But at a gig in St Louis the crowd give an ecstatic response and he observes, 'the Midwest surrenders. America is theirs'.

Both Liam and Bonehead take part in a coast to coast American phone-in interview from Minneapolis radio station Modern Rock Live on 25 February. Asked by caller Stacy in Memphis what *Wonderwall* means, Liam replies: 'It doesn't mean anything. It's a love song, innit? Whatever it means to you, you can make your own mind up on it.' Bonehead: 'And I hope it's really colourful and nice.'

Liam replies to caller Derby from upstate New York that he would have liked to have toured with The Beatles

or The Stones but would not like to go on the road with any modern-day group. He says his favourite material is 'The Beatles, The Who, The Stones, the old stuff. Jimi Hendrix, Neil Young, all that. 60s and early 70s stuff. Pistols. Burt Bacharach, all of it.' Liam says that he became a Beatles fan on hearing the likes of *Paperback writer, Helter skelter* and *Across the universe* while Bonehead namechecks *Strawberry fields*.

Liam bemoans the development of English music as being 'crap, all dance music and popping ecstasy tablets' although he is more hopeful that more and more British and American acts are 'getting back to writing songs'. He singles out Cast, Ocean Colour Scene and Smaller as his favourite new bands in Britain.

A girl called Amy from St Louis asks Liam about a recent interview where he said he does not expect to live beyond the age of 40 and asks him why. 'I don't know,' he replies. 'I've just got a feeling. I don't reckon I will. Because I'm mad and I'm off me tits and always getting off me cake.' He adds Oasis will go into the studio to record their new album later this year for release in 1997. He also points out that the crowd at gigs don't have to dance to enjoy themselves. 'People see them sitting around and go, "Oh, the crowd weren't dancing much",' he comments. 'It doesn't matter if they don't dance. As long as you're listening, everything's cool. You don't have to dance. It's not about dancing.'

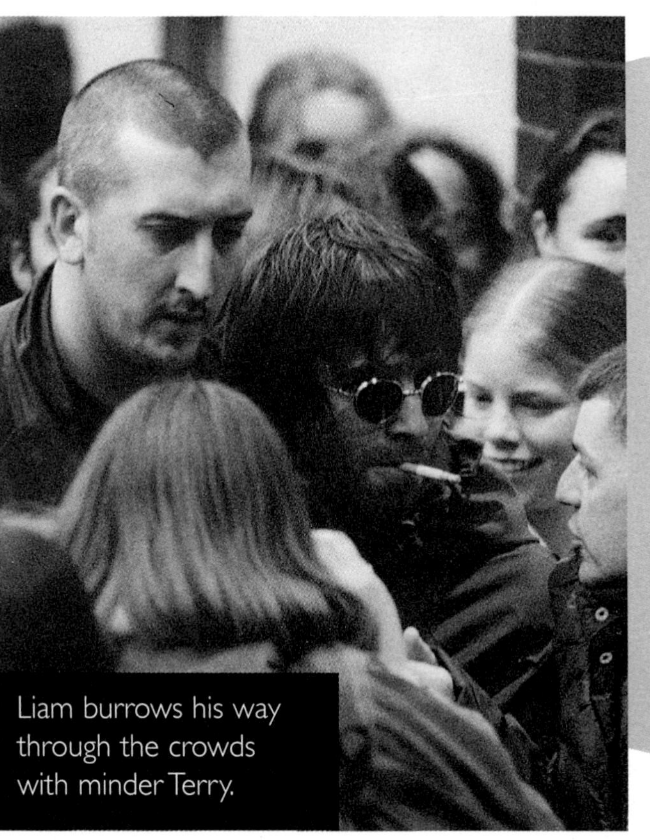

Liam burrows his way through the crowds with minder Terry.

Asked by caller Mica from Oklahoma what the meaning of (*What's the story*) *morning glory*? is, Liam surmises: 'It's meant to be a plant, innit? Morning glory? Or it's meant to be when you wake up in the morning with a rather large one on. You know what I mean? And that's where he [*Noel*] got it from, apparently. But it is a plant. I had one in my back garden, but it didn't grow above a few seeds. It's a blue climbing flower.' Bonehead: 'And it's also a rather large hard one when you wake up in the morning. Mica, you must have had one?' Liam: 'Bit of a stiffy in the morning.' Bonehead also jokes that the band's worst nightmare for the future is Liam's current beard.

On 7 March Oasis appear from Los Angeles on the major US internet site 'America online' to answer fans' questions. Liam tells one fan that Bing Crosby would support them in New York and Stevie Wonder would juggle chainsaws while Liam announces that *Champagne supernova* will be released as a single in America (it's only released as a radio promo track in the UK and Ireland).

Noel walks offstage at an outdoor show at an American ski resort on 9 March complaining it is too cold. The gig at Vernon Valley Gorge in New Jersey had been billed 'SnOasis'. Apparently Noel could not use his fingers to play the guitar as the gig progressed and almost got frostbite. At a gig in Rhode Island a boot hits Noel and lands on his guitar towards the end of one of his solo pieces. He walks offstage with Liam rushing on to berate the audience for treating him like that as he is a great songwriter.

It's 13 March and I've just flown into JFK. Oasis are in

New York tonight. They'll play the 6,000-seater Paramount theatre, which is located just underneath Madison Square Garden. The Garden is tonight playing host to the New York Rangers ice hockey team. The first and last time I'd seen a gig there was Morrissey in 1991 and the place is enormous. It can hold nearly 20,000 people seated. The Paramount's 6,000 tickets sold out within 20 minutes. The NY promoter says Oasis could have sold out the Garden twice over, such was the demand in the Big Apple.

I'm lucky to be promised a ticket for tonight's show, having failed to get one off Creation. I manage to meet up with mutual friends who work in the Oasis set-up. It's fast approaching 9 p.m. and myself and a few others are still stuck outside the venue without tickets. There are no touts. A familiar face walks up to the backstage door. It's Robbie Williams and his entourage. A couple of minutes later Patsy Kensit is also ushered through. Finally our contact arrives outside with some paste-on stickers, which allow us access to the gig and the aftershow party.

Oasis are just coming on inside to the strains of *The swamp song*. The crowd are a curious mixed bunch, lots of teenagers and 20 and 30-something couples. There's a fair sprinkling of ex-pats from Britain and Ireland. Most of the audience are seated in a C-ring around the stage. There's a VIP enclosure near the front of the stage, which also has a standing-only pit where there are about 500 fans. The reaction from fans both in the standing and seated area is warm but calm. Whereas back home fans would be inclined to stand on their seats, here they adopt a more sedate approach.

Liam stares at the audience just before *Acquiesce* kicks off and bellows, 'NYC, I see ya. Well fuckin' boo, I say.' *Supersonic* and *Hello* follow with Liam displaying his usual stage antics of leaning into the microphone with his hands behind his back; tilting over and replacing his hands on his knees; sitting down towards the front of the stage during the instrumental parts of songs. When *Some might say* starts he introduces it by saying, 'Thank God for punk rock,' while his foreword to *Some might say* is indecipherable even to trained ears used to Manc-speak. *Shakermaker* is routinely run through before the crowd begins to show some sort of life to the chorus of *Morning glory*. A big cheer rises from sections of the audience when Liam notes, 'This one's for all the people here from England because we know how to do it, man', as they launch into *Cigarettes and alcohol*. Noel unleashes an electrifying intro to *Champagne supernova* with Liam again sitting down on the stage, this time to have a drink. He leaves towards the conclusion to be followed by the rest of the band.

Noel comes back onstage to play his little acoustic set which has now become a mainstay of Oasis gigs. There's a tumultuous reception as he strums the first few chords of *Wonderwall*, but he's just kidding and smiles as he plays *Whatever* instead. Then the crowd get what they want and he plays *Wonderwall*. Unfortunately, for such a classic song this seems like a throwaway treatment of an epic track which at least should have the whole band on accompaniment with perhaps a string quartet thrown in for good measure. And Noel is not half as good as his brother on lead vocals to the number, although the fans do not seem to mind as they effortlessly sing along. Next up is *Slide away* which Noel dedicates to his old mate Richard Ashcroft (The Verve having split up several months ago now). The rest of the band reappear to join in *Don't look back in anger* before Liam finally makes his way out to take the lead vocals on *I am the walrus*. The band exits and *Helter skelter* comes over the PA. Strangely, it appeared to be a muted gig, one of those off-nights or perhaps there was too much anti-climax on my part.

About 100 people stand around with their aftershow stickers and are told to wait in the front row seats. Eventually, we make our way backstage. Noel is still hanging around near banks of electrical equipment and we follow the group leaders into an upstairs room. Cold beer is laid out in boxes of ice. Most of the people here are from Manchester and London with a small number of Americans. I fortuitously bump into a friend from Dublin who's with a group of Irish people living in New York. He tells me the place to be is the Irish Bar after the show as that's where the party's going to be. He had been in the bar the day before and Liam was there seated all alone. Unlike most backstage parties there's a general air of unpretentiousness at this one and eventually Bonehead, Alan and Guigsy make their way in to polish off the remaining beers in the ice bucket. There's no sign of Liam or Noel.

And so to the Irish Bar. It's located just a couple of hundred yards from the hotel where Oasis are staying. There's a couple of hundred people inside but it's not too uncomfortable. I get talking to a girl and suddenly Bonehead comes up. We get chatting and he admits he's looking forward to playing the Dublin dates next week. A friend of his asks him if I'm from Manchester. 'No, he's from Ireland,' Bonehead replies. Noel arrives, comes wandering through the crowd followed by a few hangers-on and makes his way to the very back of the bar where Evan Dando and Robbie Williams are holding court. Bizarrely, Metallica drummer Lars Ulrich is a big Oasis fan and he's here too, propping up the bar.

I make my way to several people I know at the front of the bar near the door and spot Liam stumbling through as he tries to make his way over. It's the first time I've seen him so close and the first impression is his height. His beard is now quite unruly and he's also sporting round glasses. He apparently thinks this image makes him look more like his hero John Lennon, but his mother complains it makes him look far older than his actual age. He appears slightly disorientated and incoherent. Liam is accompanied by the main Oasis bodyguard, Terry, a London skinhead who's apparently 6 feet 7 inches and certainly looks it. Liam stalls near the door and says a few words to one or two of my party whom he's familiar with. Our eyes meet and I say 'Hello' and he gives a courteous nod. With that he's out the door, no doubt back to the hotel where Patsy's waiting for him.

One of the people I'm with announces he's off to the Limelight Club – complete with half an ecstasy tablet Liam has just given him. Shortly afterwards I make my excuses and leave as the clock approaches 3 a.m., with the Oasis crew only just beginning to get into the swing of things.

While in America Noel's infamous big mouth lands him into another pool of hot water. In the 23 March issue of *Melody Maker* he gives an explosive interview to writer Ben Stud. Noel is pictured on the cover of the magazine dressed in a duffel coat and holding a bottle of Heineken with the beaming headline: 'You lookin' at me, pal? Oasis get stroppy in the USA.' The interview had been conducted in Philadelphia on 9 March. He admits for the first time that it is important Oasis break America. 'Cos we can't really go round saying we're the greatest band in the world if America doesn't know who the fuck we are,' he points out. He also denies suggestions that they're ripping off The Beatles and stresses 'to some people who are 15 or 16 we're better than The Beatles . . . The Jam and The Smiths in the 80s were my fuckin' Beatles.'

But it's part two of the interview printed in the 30 March issue of *Melody Maker* which causes a public outcry among the usual pathetic Tory do-gooders and even warrants a police investigation. It's not even the drugs reference which results in grief. He admits most of his songs are written while he's under the influence of one thing or another, but never cannabis which he describes as a mind-wasting drug. He warns kids not to do drugs as he points out at least he can afford to. 'Drugs may look like a fuckin' way out, but at the end of the day all they do is make the problem worse,' he insists. And it's the following quote which causes a storm: 'What people have to understand is that we are, er, lads,' he explains. 'We have burgled houses and nicked car stereos, and we all like girls and we swear and I go to football and take the piss.'

Trouble rears its ugly head and on 23 March Dr Adrian Rogers of the Conservative Family Institute calls for an Oasis boycott due to their drugs and crime-ridden past. He appears on ITV's morning show *GMTV* and decries Oasis's 'yobbish, criminal behaviour'. Several daily papers pick up on the burglary claims and Manchester police announce they are investigating them following complaints. One reporter from the *Sunday Mirror* approaches Liam at Manchester airport as he arrives in on a flight with Patsy Kensit and asks him about the allegations. Liam jokes they are true and he has another 'job' lined up. 'Yes, I'm doing another one tonight and it could

be your house,' he smirks. Asked if he is worried about the police probe, he replies: 'I'm not bothered, I'm mad for it.'

His mother Peggy is quoted by the *Guardian* as saying: 'Noel only moved out when he was 23. As far as I know he was never involved in any crime. They were just normal boys. They are thoughtful and kind and all they think about are their family and friends.'

Manchester CID Chief Superintendent David James speaks formally to *Melody Maker* writer Ben Stud about Noel's burglary allegations. Stud tells him he does not think Noel meant the claims to be taken seriously. Noel had previously admitted he got probation as a teenager for robbing a local corner store and that could be all that's to his boast.

Oasis's American triumph as the biggest British band to hit that country in decades was visibly highlighted on 2 May when they attained perhaps one of the pinnacles of any band's career achievements by appearing as the cover story in *Rolling Stone*. A bearded Liam and Noel are pictured with the headline: 'Oasis: They're hard-drinking, groupie-shagging, drug-snorting louts. They're the Gallagher brothers. And they're huge.' Asked by writer Chris Mundy, who conducts the interview just after the Brits, whether those words are true Noel replied dead-pan, 'Yeah.'

Guigsy gives a rare insight into his own personality: 'I don't really do anything. I don't fight now, but I used to be a bad one, just punching people. I used to have a temper, but I don't no more. Now I just sit in the corner and light up (normally marijuana). Watching football is my main hobby. Watching football, watching videos about football, reading about football and talking about football. That's pretty much all I care about.'

Asked does he ever get tired of being full of shit, Liam coyly replies: 'No, I love hearing myself talk.'

And we love hearing him sing.

The Maine Attraction

Oasis arrive early in the week in Ireland for two sell-out shows at Dublin's The Point on 22 and 23 March. The Irish media go into overdrive in their build-up to the gigs and even though perhaps the most popular band in the world is from and lives in, Dublin-U2-Oasis are being treated as heir apparent to the throne.

On the night before the gig Liam is in Kehoe's bar in South Anne Street. He's accompanied by an unidentified young Irish woman. In the back lounge he immediately notices Michael Hutchence, of all people, sitting at the bar. Liam goes over to him and puts his face into Hutchence's and growls. The INXS star is a regular visitor to Dublin and his band were recording a new album in the city's Windmill Lane studio at the time. The *Daily Star* in Britain and even many of the music papers reported that the 'bust-up' was broken up by Bono. But friends who were in the bar at the time of the encounter say the U2 singer was not even there. He did, however, meet up with the band at the Pod nightclub and is pictured outside the nightspot with Liam, who has his tongue out as the two feign a snogging scene. The picture appears on the front page of the following day's *Evening Herald* and most of the British magazines in later weeks.

Liam had said before that he once met Bono backstage at the MTV awards and gave out to the U2 star for saying to him 'All right, my son', with Liam pointing out that Bono is not his father. Noel has always admitted U2 are one of his favourite bands and once revealed that he met Bono at a club in London the previous autumn and was amazed when Bono spontaneously sang the whole of *Slide away* to him word-perfect and without being prompted. He also discloses he cried when he heard U2's *One* for the first time.

During Thursday he and a lot of the Oasis crew pop into their favourite pub in Dublin, Bruxelles, and at one stage Liam is spotted dancing on the table in the downstairs bar. Writer and DJ Paulo Hewitt spun some discs there for the band while they were in town. Hewitt co-wrote a biography on Paul Weller and has been commissioned by Oasis to write the official biography on the band for release next year. Apparently, Noel has requested that no pictures be used with its text.

Tickets for the Friday show were fetching up to £200 on the black market. Originally costing £14.50 (remarkably cheap, but Oasis instruct promoters to keep costs down for the fans) they are eventually forced down to £40 with half an hour to go before Oasis are due onstage.

The band hired a private plane to bring over family and friends from Manchester. Most of their cousins and relatives based in Ireland have also travelled up for the weekend. The band themselves are staying in the upmarket city centre Westbury Hotel, with Liam signing himself in as 'Lucifer' and Noel as 'Jesus'.

Their Friday gig is much the same running order as the New York set with *Round are way* a new addition. The most emotional part of the show happens when Noel starts the chords to *Wonderwall* and all he gets to sing is the opening word of the song before the 8,500-strong crowd sing the whole song word-perfect. Noel is visibly moved and thanks the fans before being whisked from The Point to the RTE TV studios across the city in Donnybrook. He appears on *The Late Late Show*, having been persuaded by his mother, who's a big fan of chat-show king Gay Byrne. Noel performs *Wonderwall* and *Live forever* to an enraptured studio audience. The show is repeated on Channel 4.

Noel admits the response from the Dublin show was one of his most thrilling moments. 'Judging by the crowd's reaction I think it was one of the best gigs we've ever played, really,' he says. 'It's the crowd that makes a show for us 'cause we don't do that much on stage, we sort of stand around and play the music and if the crowd are up for it, then we are and let's just say they were

made for it tonight.'

As for dealing with fame: 'Well, we've not had time to sit down and think about it. I suppose if we sat down and thought about what's happened over the last two years we'd probably be "in the big house", as me Nana says! But we're too busy working, too busy, in the eye of the hurricane, which is the calmest place. Tonight going to the gig we had to have a police escort and all around the car were little kids' faces and I was more nervous for them in case they got run over than I was for me, in case they got hold of me! I'm quite lucky to have a great family and a great bunch of friends around who are . . . if they find that you might be getting ideas above your station and start being big-headed and believe your own press they'll sort of take you to one side and remind you where you came from. So I suppose that's a great leveller.'

Asked by a member of the audience how long he sees 'it lasting' he replies: 'As long as it lasts! I don't think you can predict the future or anything like that. I suppose if you look back at The Beatles, they said, "Oh, we won't be anywhere in ten years", they all wanted to run hairdressing salons or whatever, but The Beatles are still going strong after 30 years, still releasing records. I just hope it lasts for as long as I'm enjoying it and if I'm not enjoying it, I hope somebody gives me the sack!' As for the worry about drying up: 'I think it's an ongoing concern of artists, if you got up one day and weren't able to write a song, I suppose your lifeblood's gone. But you could always go to the pub and drown your sorrows! It's hard work, but it's not as hard as some of the jobs I've had, you just take it as it comes.'

He finishes the interview by signing a copy of (*What's the story*) *morning glory*? for a member of the audience who fortuitously has a copy there. He ends by singing an enthralling version of *Live forever*.

Saturday's gig comes along and again it's pretty much the same set. That evening the press are technically barred from the gig but I manage to go up to the local promoter at a portacabin outside the venue and gently persuade him to give me a ticket as I'm due to review the Manic Street Preachers for *Melody Maker*. Inside, I bump into a friend whose sister works in the Westbury. Chaos had been the order of the day at the hotel that morning and word was fast spreading about the early morning shenanigans. Liam and Patsy had a major bust-up in the hotel around 5 a.m. He had been at the bar chatting to a pretty-looking young woman and kissing her. Some British tabloids reported the woman was former *Brookside* actress Anna Friel, who played Beth Jordache, but in actual fact it was Dubliner Eilish Ni Bhriain (25). An enraged Patsy saw what was going on and ticked Liam off. He was having none of it and hurled a stream of four-letter abuse at her, called her a 'stupid woman' and told her to go to bed. A tearful Patsy promptly fled up the stairs and deposited Liam's clothes out the hotel window. He followed her up some time later and a screaming match between the two followed. She asked for, and was given, another room by the management. Liam promptly trashed the room, kicking in the TV set and slammed a lamp against a wall. Although the hotel would later deny the room had been damaged, sources within the Westbury say the repair bill came to £2,500. It was added to the band's £8,000 room bill for their stay. Patsy took one of the first flights out of Dublin back to London and found comfort in estranged husband Jim Kerr. The Simple Minds singer reportedly said on hearing of her treatment at the hands of Liam, 'I'll fly to Ireland and sort Gallagher out.'

Eilish Ni Bhriain later told the Irish newspaper *Sunday World*: 'We had a lovely time together and he's a good kisser, but it was far too seedy. As we were kissing he was trying to pull my trousers off. When Patsy went to bed Liam came back over to me, but people who knew her were trying to get him away from me. I got fed up and went to ring a taxi. I was on the phone when he pulled me into the toilets.'

She first met Liam in Bruxelles bar and got the impression he was already arguing with Patsy. The two were soon holding hands and kissing. 'He kept trying to get me to go somewhere private,' she claims. 'He couldn't go back to his hotel because Patsy was there. When I said I wouldn't sleep with him he asked why and I laughed and said I was a nice Catholic Irish girl. I don't mind kissing him, but anything else just wasn't my scene.

Noel at Slane July 1995.

He couldn't believe that I refused and told me that no other girl had ever refused him. I basically said, "Tough" . . . as kisses go on a scale of one to ten he's about an eight. I've kissed a lot worse.'

That Sunday's *News of the World* splashed with a story headlined 'Patsy's having Oasis star's baby', with an outlandish tale about how Liam always wanted to be a father.

After the Saturday gig I wrangled my way to the backstage party. The usual Dublin social liggers and hangers-on are around but Oasis stay in the Green Room annexe of The Point where most of their close relatives are being entertained. Just Guigsy and Bonehead eventually come out of the cocoon to join the main party.

Afterwards, myself, an Irish DJ and one of Noel's closest Irish cousins gatecrash a party U2 have thrown for Oasis in a closed-off VIP bar in the Kitchen nightclub, which is owned by the Irish supergroup. On going to the toilets there's a familiar figure hunched just inside the door having an argument about football with an Irish Manchester United fan. The following Monday's Irish edition of the *Daily Mirror* splashed with a story headlined 'Liam beaten up in U2 club'. It reported that Liam had been beaten up by a football hooligan and kicked to the ground before being led away bleeding up a backstairs. But no such incident obviously occurred and it would have been very hard, as Liam was accompanied by two bodyguards, one of them being Bono's personal minder. Back in the VIP bar there's not much sign of any of the Oasis lads and I briefly got talking to Paul 'Bod' Gallagher and say hello to Guigsy who's standing at the main entrance to the club.

The early hours of the morning following the second gig again see eventful happenings in the Westbury. The *News of the World* has brought over the Gallaghers' father, Tommy, to Dublin to meet up with them after all those years. Tommy is being paid a decent sum by the tabloid and books into the hotel. That morning he decides to search for his long-lost sons in the hotel foyer. Liam immediately spots him and, accompanied by a couple of minders, lunges over towards him. He pushes his sunglasses to the end of his nose and screams, 'I told you I'd break your fucking legs.' As he tries to hit Tommy he's pulled back by a minder. Liam starts bouncing up and down and taunts his dad, 'Are you ready for a fight?' before sneering, 'I'm a millionaire, you loser. I can afford bail now.' Tommy replies by joking, 'I'll fight you if you promise not to kiss me.' He then inflames the situation by remarking, 'Get Patsy Henshit [*sic*] to calm you down. Stop acting like a silly boy.' Liam responds by saying, 'Your legs have gone,' while Tommy points out, 'You couldn't break Percy Sugden's legs.'

Tommy later surmises: 'He looked like he wanted to kill me. I'm seriously worried about Liam. This rock star thing has sent him off the rails. He went crazy and tried to cripple me, his own father. He needs help, and soon.'

The next afternoon Liam, on arrangement, calls up Tommy's room. The *News of the World* reporter Jane Atkinson picks up the phone. This is how the conversation, which was taped, went . . . Reporter: 'Hello.' Liam: 'Hello, yeah, who's that?' Reporter; 'It's Jane, a friend of Tommy's. Who's speaking?' Liam: 'Put him on.' Reporter: 'Hold on.' Tommy: 'Hello.' Liam: 'Hello.' Tommy: 'Liam?' Liam: 'Yeah.' Tommy: 'It's your dad.' Liam: 'Yeah.' Tommy: 'How are you keeping?' Liam: 'I'm all right, how are you?' Tommy: 'I'm up for the concert, but couldn't get a ticket.' Liam: 'Yeah, you're not going to get a ticket. If I catch you round, walking around the lobby in this hotel, you're going to get your legs fucking broke. Right? See ya later.' With that Liam slams down the phone. Tommy is shocked and rings Liam up again only for his son to bang down the phone again when he discovers who it is.

Tommy explains: 'All I wanted to do was explain that I was proud of him. I thought it was time we healed the old wounds. I've missed them. I worked hard for them and they repaid me by telling lies about me to refuel their hard men image. The only mental torture I gave them was to ground them if they came in late. I was a father figure, that's all. I went to Ireland as a peacemaker, all they want to do is break my heart.'

When I phoned Tommy up at his home in Burnage he seemed genuinely aggrieved at the fall-out and remarked, 'It's like Ulster, too much fighting and not enough talking.'

The *News of the World* tracked down other members

of the Gallagher family in Duleek, Co. Meath. Their granny, Annie, is quoted as saying: 'I'm so proud of Noel and Liam, but they've never been in touch for years. They haven't sent me Christmas or birthday cards. The only time I see them is in the newspaper. It's very hurtful. They were all happy as a family but then they denied it all.'

An aunt, Kathleen, claims she went into hospital for chemotherapy for leukaemia in 1992 and most of the Gallaghers, except Noel and Liam, agreed to be tested to see if they were a match for her bone marrow. 'They were lovely, affectionate boys and would always give me a kiss and a cuddle before going to bed,' she recalls. 'Luckily, my youngest brother Dominica was able to be my donor and I had a transplant. It was a terrible time for the family. Noel didn't come and see me, though he did send a message. But I never heard from Liam.'

While in Ireland Noel gives few interviews to local newspapers, although he does talk to Gayle Killilea of the *Sunday Independent*. 'I don't know what true love is,' he ponders, 'but let's put it this way; in about 30 years time I would put money on still being with Meg. The thing about some people is that they always think that the grass is greener on the other side.' As for Liam: 'Liam is in love with himself. Liam loves himself so much he can't love another person. You have to give love to receive love, and if you're not willing to give you can't expect to get. He'll never fall in love. To be frank, he's been like that since the day he appeared on the cover of a magazine.'

He also gives an indication of where the future lies: 'It's inevitable that Oasis will break up one day. We're not going to go on forever like The Rolling Stones. The day I go solo I could definitely see myself in the mould of Paul Weller, with a band and me singing, so if, and when, Oasis break up I'm not going to sit on my arse. Or maybe I will. I'm the luckiest man in the world. I've got my music, I've got a place to live, I've a Rolls-Royce I'm driven around in. I've plenty of money, Meg and my family. I'm not searching for anything. I'm just searching for the perfect pop song.'

He also gives an interesting insight into his own mind-set to *Hot Press*'s Joe Jackson. 'Critics in Britain are so bitter because I write the simplest of pop songs that any-

one could write, the simplest lyrics,' he says. 'The four members of the band [sic], we're not musically adept. So some people don't like us because of the success we've had. They feel they could do it themselves. But I will not make any apologies for the fact that people come to our concerts to sing along. All I've got to say to critics is, "Stick to your poxy, fucking job, then look at me when I'm on the *David Letterman Show* because I'm selling shitloads of records and stick that in your pipe and smoke it, you fucker."'

He adds: 'I'm from a working-class background and when I look out and see the audience that's me there. And when the audience look at me, that's them up there they see. I'm not no fuckin' icon or whatever those commentators would like me to be. I'm just some shitkicker from Manchester, who got a good break. I'm no John Lennon. I'm just some shitkicker who's shit at football, decided to play a guitar and has written a few good songs. That's the bottom line as far as I'm concerned. Anyone can sit in front of me and say, "You're the new John Lennon" and I won't disagree. But fuck that, I don't feel I am. There's no one could touch that man. The one person who is close to him but still couldn't touch him was his mate Paul McCartney.'

As for his drug habit: 'I don't preach to anybody, man. If people ask me a question I give them an answer. But if any kid was to walk up to me in the street and say, "I'm thinking of doing drugs". I'd say, "You wanna go home, get in the fucking shower, have a cold one and think of this: in 30 years from now you'll wish you didn't." Because if I knew what I know now, I wouldn't have even started smoking, because even if I don't get run over by a bus, I'm hardly likely to reach 65, am I?'

Noel once said he knows how it feels to be poor and not being able to afford to pay into see his favourite bands. 'I was on the dole and I got 17 fucking pounds a week to live on and, as I say, I remember that too fucking well. Every day . . . some days when I'm walking up the high street in Camden nothing'll fucking bother me, but other days, there'll be kids, 15, 16, living on the streets, saying, "Got any spare change, mate?" and I'll literally go to the bank for them. But then I think, "What the fuck am

I giving them money for?" But part of it is because I know that by the grace of God I never got that far . . . And I do sometimes feel guilty about what I have, think "Do I deserve all this?", though then again I say, "Why not, I've worked hard for what I have." Look at it this way, I just bought a fucking million-pound house [*believed to be in London's St John's Wood*]. A million-pound house! And I'm thinking, "That fucking thing cost me a million and there are kids living on the streets." But then again, I'll remember that I earned that money and realise that I am an artist. I do, as I said earlier, give pleasure to millions of people and this is how they choose to reward me. That's fucking life, man, and this is the way it's worked out for me.'

Meanwhile, back to the Liam and Patsy saga. When Liam is later asked by a reporter with the *Daily Mirror* if Patsy is pregnant he scoffs, 'If she is it's not mine', and adds, 'There's already enough Gallaghers running about in this world.'

Liam's trail of destruction around Europe continues after his sojourn in Dublin. The English tabloid press report he trashed a £200-a-night suite in Grenoble's luxury Park Hotel after a night on the town. Another claims the Hilton Hotel in Milan refused to allow him to bring a teenage girl up to his room after a £500 band binge at the bar. Hotel manager Bruno Manca is quoted as saying, 'She was only 17 and I would have lost my licence.' Liam met up with Patsy again in Barcelona, having patched things up with her. 'We are still an item. We always were,' he points out. She later accompanies him at their Manchester gigs, turns up at a celebrity football match with him in May and the same month he surprises her in Munich by handing her the keys to a £78,000 sports car he bought for her. She gets the name 'Liam' and a shamrock tattooed onto one of her ankles while he gets 'Patsy' tattooed onto his right shoulder.

During the first week of April both Paul Weller and Noel Gallagher spend some time recording B-sides with Ocean Colour Scene. Later that month both Liam and Noel show up in London and support the band as a surprise when they play under the moniker 'The Gallagher Brothers'. They perform acoustic versions of *Wonderwall*, *Cast no shadow*, *Live forever* and join Ocean Colour Scene for an encore of The Beatles' *Day tripper*.

Noel also provides vocals for a new Chemical Brothers' single. It's believed to be called *Tomorrow never Noels* after The Beatles' track *Tomorrow never knows*. His alliance with the dance act finds little favour with Liam who describes them as 'non-imaginative bollocks keyboards'.

Noel appears on Chris Evans's *TFI Friday* Channel 4 show on 5 April. He has been under police scrutiny about claims he burgled houses and jokes that he's just been casing a few joints before he adds in the word 'allegedly'. He announces that he has finished writing two new songs, one which we already know as *My big mouth* and the other titled *I hope, I think, I know*, which is perhaps the melodious new love song he penned in America.

They head back to North America in the second week of April for some more dates. But on 10 April controversy again strikes when they pull out of a gig at the Pacific Coliseum in Vancouver after they play barely half their set to a 8,000-strong crowd. Coins had rained onstage for much of the show and a shoe eventually hit Noel in the face. Liam shouts that the band aren't 'fucking monkeys' but 'the best band in the world'.

The band is forced to cancel dates in Los Angeles and Phoenix as Noel is treated for suspected tonsillitis. While in America he talks with Burt Bacharach about writing a song together. Noel has been a longtime fan of Burt's, whose best known tracks were the 60s hits *Do you know the way to San Jose?*, *Walk on by* and *Say a little prayer*. Burt remarks on Oasis: 'It's really good listening. It's not hard for me to go through that tape [*Morning glory*] because I found it pretty creative. They set a very good wide sound, the tracks feel very good. Liam's voice is very unusual.'

Oasis's lawyers also take action against an 'Oasis FC' fan club, claiming fans may get the impression it's an official group. The club is wound up on 18 April.

Judge Mr Justice Hannon announces he will soon begin hearing the Tony McCarroll case. The judge admits he has never heard of Oasis, but then in previous cases he had never heard of the likes of Bruce Springsteen, UB40 or Paul 'Gazza' Gascoigne.

Both Liam and Noel appear on the front page of the one-off glossy-covered 70th anniversary special *Melody Maker* on 27 April. Noel is pictured by photographer Tom Sheehan holding up his hand with the words 'Beatles 67–70' scrawled in paint across his palm. The other three members of the band are pictured on the back page of the magazine. Liam says he's happy with Noel being the lyricist and he will stay a singer for the foreseeable future, pointing out Elvis Presley never wrote any songs. He admits The Sex Pistols are his second favourite group next to The Beatles. Noel reveals he went to a Harley Street specialist about his ears and in the waiting-room was Jason Donovan and Craig McLachlan (from *Neighbours* and *Grease*). He discloses that the band has cut down on its cocaine use and he has given up cannabis as it decreased his blood pressure, causing him dizziness and breathing difficulties. He also predicts that Oasis will realistically release five albums while he'd also like to form a supergroup at some stage with Paul Weller, Johnny Marr and Reni from The Stone Roses.

Ironically, the *NME* of the same week has Blur's Damon Albarn on its cover. He admits he obtained a copy of *Morning glory* and played it while he was in the gym. 'I've learned a few things from Liam, definitely,' he tells writer Johnny Cigarettes. 'I've learned nothing from Noel. Liam is that band, completely. He's the reason people love them so much. He's got a real star quality about him. But there are sides of them which are so alien to me that they're not even worth talking about . . . I couldn't write something like *Wonderwall*. I couldn't bring myself to write simple stuff like that. It's not in my nature. Why on earth would I want to?' Obviously, Damon has lately neglected to listen to his own lyrics of *Country house* and *Girls and boys*.

And so to Oasis's homecoming gigs in Manchester on 22 and 23 April. The city is abuzz with apprehension and excitement as Maine Road plays host to its home-town heroes and the biggest band in Britain while across town Old Trafford is the setting for Manchester United's last home game of the season, a game against Nottingham Forest; if they win convincingly they'll be almost certain of winning the championship (they win 5–0). The Sunday show at Maine Road was the first gig to sell out and the Saturday concert was added due to demand. I couldn't get a ticket for Saturday but I am assured of one for Sunday. I spend Saturday in Liverpool where I get to see the 'Pool against Middlesbrough for Ian Rush's last game with the Reds. Later that night I hit Cream nightclub but bizarrely manage to get my luggage stolen, having stashed it in a laneway outside when the club closed (yes, there was drink taken!). And so the first train to Manchester at 8.30 a.m. and a trip to the Argyle Centre for a new bag, change of clothing and other necessities.

I'm booked into the Midland Holiday Inn Crown Plaza but unfortunately have to wait from 12.10 p.m. 'till 3 p.m. to get a room and have to endure a lobby full of Manchester United fans. Worse still was to happen as certain record company personnel did not leave tickets as promised and after much haranguing on mobile phones I eventually get one for my mate from Dublin. We leave with another friend from Liverpool and arrive at the ground at 8.15 p.m. More persuasion is necessary to unleash another ticket from the organisers after much pleading and name-dropping.

But it's bedlam outside the ground, the worst-policed concert I've ever been to. Stewards seem to be losing control of the situation as scallies, teenage urchins and ticketless locals try to force their way into the ground. I even spot one enterprising group using a ladder to get over the walls. Crazily, there's just one turnstile open and it's pandemonium trying to get through. After over half an hour of panic we eventually track down a helpful security man who whispers to us to follow him. He arranges for a turnstile to be quickly opened specially for us and a half dozen others. We finally get into the ground 40 minutes into Oasis's set. But we were lucky and many fans with tickets did not even get in. Several fans had been beaten up outside the ground earlier that day by louts who snatched their tickets. A steward was knocked unconscious by a baying mob. The police later pleaded innocence and said it was up to the organisers to provide security around the ground (no doubt if it was an anti-poll tax march or something similar they'd be well out in force).

The set itself had started off with the deafening sound of helicopter rotor blades before the familiar strains of *The swamp song* and its lead into *Acquiesce*. The next few tracks (in no particular order) follow the trend from New York and Dublin: *Supersonic, Champagne supernova, Cigarettes and alcohol, Morning glory, Round are way* (which has replaced *Hey now* from the American tour), *Whatever, Hello, Some might say, Roll with it, Cast no shadow* and *The masterplan* (which was omitted from the US leg). The first full song I catch is *Some might say*. For *Live forever* a giant backdrop displays pictures of great stars who've gone to rock 'n' roll heaven: Elvis . . . Janis Joplin . . . Sid Vicious . . . Bob Marley . . . Jimi Hendrix . . . and finally, John Lennon. Liam turns to the image and bows in honour. A mini-orchestra adds to the magnificence of it all.

For *Wonderwall* Liam and Noel appear to have an argument over who should sing it. Liam wins out, with Noel strumming along on his Union Jack emblazoned guitar while he takes over on *Don't look back in anger*. They end with *I am the walrus* before coming back for Slade's *Cum on feel the noize* (Noddy Holder is in attendance to see the cover version of his song). And so the 40,000-strong crowd makes its way out after one of the most spectacular and passionate gigs ever witnessed in this town. Sadly, there's more trouble outside with several fans beaten up by rampaging thugs.

Manchester is awash with celebrities for the Oasis show. Among those putting in appearances are Caroline 'Mrs Merton' Hook, Angus Deayton (who travelled up from and back to London by taxi), Julia Carling, Joe Strummer of The Clash, Terry Christian, Alex Higgins, Johnny Marr and a couple of the *Brookside* and *Coronation Street* cast members. Several players from Man Utd also show up, including Ryan Giggs, Lee Sharpe, Gary Pallister and Gary Neville with Noel agreeing they can have tickets as he buries the hatchet somewhat with the players (a rumoured altercation between Liam and Giggs at a club with Liam allegedly saying 'You're a shit footballer' is played down by Sharpe who says the two got on fine). Most of the Man City squad, including Georgiou Kinkladze, also put in an appearance.

Myself and my mates decide to try out the famous 'Dry Bar', scene of Liam's drunken carry-on last year. It's closed and we ask how to get to the Hacienda. It's our first time there and we're surprised it's so small, only to be told that the part open tonight is the 'cocktail bar' end of the club and the main cavernous area is closed. Rumours spread that Noel may call in but he fails to show up and the only person of any note we can make out is Nottingham Forest's Stuart Pearce.

Back at the hotel I get into a long chat with James Dean Bradfield of the Manic Street Preachers and for some reason think I've mislaid a mobile phone at the Hacienda. It's past three a.m. and the place is surely closed but I ask the porter can I get out. And who walks in through the door but Noel. He's on his own and I introduce myself and we talk about his cousins in Ireland. He leaves but several minutes later as we're stumbling off to bed Noel comes out of a lift. A mate says, 'Are you playing Ireland again?' He replies, 'Yeah, we're playing Cork in July.' I point out the only aspect of the show I was disappointed with tonight was Noel's Union Jack guitar and remonstrate with him. He gives a V-sign with his fingers, mutters, 'Fuck off', and walks off into the night.

The next day we decide to take a trip out to Burnage. This tale gets sadder as the address we were given by a local Manc we got chatting to in the Hacienda was for '21 Cromwell Grove, Burnage'. Such a road exists about two miles from Burnage but it was only on closer inspection we discovered the canny Manc had meant to write down '21 Cromwell Road', the home of Fred and Rosemary West in Gloucester. We ask some locals do they know where the Gallaghers live and make our way back to Burnage. But we still can't find the house and time is running out fast. We decide to get a cab to the nearest train station for a connection to Piccadilly and onwards to the airport. There'd be dreams of Oasis playing Loch Lomond in Scotland, Knebworth in England and Cork in Ireland in August. We'd seen Oasis in their home town, met Noel and even staked out their stomping ground of Burnage. As we descend the steps to the platform the sign had just one word of graffiti scrawled across it: 'Oasis'. No doubt the same slogan is scribbled on train stations across the world by starry-eyed kids, hoping that some day they too may take a roller-coaster ride to a destination which reads fame and fortune.

DISCOGRAPHY

Date	Title	Highest Chart Position
Singles		
11/ 4/94	Supersonic	31
20/ 6/94	Shakermaker	11
8/ 8/94	Live forever	10
9/10/94	Cigarettes and alcohol	7
19/12/94	Whatever	3
24/ 3/95	Some might say	1
14/ 8/95	Roll with it	2
30/10/95	Wonderwall	2
19/ 2/96	Don't look back in anger	1
Albums		
30/ 8/94	Definitely maybe	1
2/10/95	(What's the story) morning glory?	1

Information on Oasis can also be obtained on the Internet by using the following pages:

What's the story? http://www.staff.dircon.net/michael/oasis/

Oasisteria http//www.staff.dircon.net/michael/oasis

Official Oasis http//www.oasisnet. com

Oasis, they're the fucking bollox
http//www.users.dircon.co.uk/–neil/oasis.htm

Creation records homepage http://www.music

Official Oasis fan club:
Freepost CV744
3 Alveston Place
Leamington Spa
CV32 4BR
England